ALL THE
RIGHT
MOVES

ALL THE RIGHT MOVES

A Guide to Crafting Breakthrough Strategy

CONSTANTINOS C. MARKIDES

HARVARD BUSINESS SCHOOL PRESS   Boston, Massachusetts

Printed in the United States of America

05 06   9

Library of Congress Cataloging-in-Publication Data
Markides, Constantinos C.
   All the right moves : a guide to crafting breakthrough strategy /
Constantinos C. Markides
       p.   cm.
   Includes index.
   ISBN 0-87584-833-8 (alk. paper)
   1. Strategic planning. 2. Technological innovations—Economic
aspects. I. Title.
   HD30.28.M3536 1999
658.4'012—dc21   99-32401
                                                                      CIP

*The paper used in this publication meets the requirements of the American
National Standard for Permanence of Paper for Publications and
Documents in Libraries and Archives Z39.48-1992.*

Contents

113043

Preface

In early 1988, the newly appointed CEO of the small Danish bank Lan & Spar was under pressure to rejuvenate his financially troubled organization. Peter Schou had taken over as CEO at a particularly bad time: deregulation of the Danish banking industry in the mid-1980s had led to mergers, consolidations, and turbulence in the industry. Despite being more than one hundred years old, Lan & Spar was hit hard by the changes in its environment and was in danger of going bankrupt.

Schou had been working in the industry since the age of sixteen. All those years in banking, however, did not make the job he had to do any easier. He knew that the bank's current strategy was not working. He also knew that it was up to him to develop a new one. But what, exactly, should go into the new strategy? And how should he go about developing it?

If Schou had turned to an academic for help, it is unlikely that he would have received much useful guidance. Despite the obvious importance of a superior strategy to the success of an organization, and despite decades of academic research on the subject, there is little agreement among academics as to what strategy really is. Nor could Schou have expected too much help from other CEOs or managers. If asked, most practicing executives would have defined strategy as "the actions you take to achieve your company's objectives." Although technically correct, this definition is so general as to be virtually meaningless.

Needless to say, this state of affairs is unfortunate. Undoubtedly, part of the confusion is self-inflicted. But a major portion of the problem results from a genuine lack of understanding among managers and academics about the content of strategy. We simply do not know what strategy really is or how to develop a good one.

This book is concerned with the art and craft of creating strategy. It takes the perspective of a senior manager who is about to develop a new strategy for his or her organization and explores the thinking process that this manager should go through to create an innovative new strategy. It therefore asks the twofold question, "What issues should this manager address in thinking about a new strategy, and how should he or she think about them?"

Despite the seeming simplicity of this question, it addresses one of the most controversial issues in management today. People seem to disagree about almost every aspect of strategy making that this question raises: they disagree about which issues to address in developing strategy, they disagree about the process of developing strategy, and they even disagree as to whether one can "think" about strategy at all.

In this book, I propose an answer to this question that is based on my research of the past three years. A variety of companies have been the focus of this research, all of them strategic innovators in their industries. These are companies whose strategies have not only been fundamentally different from those of their competitors but have also turned out to be tremendously successful. By studying these successful innovators, I believe we can develop a deeper understanding of what accounts for the making of innovative strategies.

I've observed that there are certain simple but fundamental principles underlying every successful strategy. When one goes beyond the surface differences in such strategies and probes deeper into their roots, one cannot fail but notice that all successful strategies share the same underlying principles. Thus, the principles of Microsoft's successful strategy are essentially the same as those which propelled Sears to industry leadership one hundred years ago. My argument is that by understanding these basic principles, any manager can use them to design a successful strategy.

Still, designing a successful strategy is not a science—it is an art. It is the art of asking intelligent questions, of exploring possible answers, of experimenting with possible solutions, and of starting the thinking process all over again by questioning the answers arrived at a year or two before. Effective strategic thinking is the process of continually asking questions and thinking through the issues in a creative way. Thus, correctly formulating the questions is often more important than finding a "solution," thinking through an issue from a variety of angles is often more productive than collecting and analyzing unlimited data, and actually experimenting with new ideas is often more productive than conducting extensive analysis and discussion.

Designing a successful strategy is also a never-ending quest. Just because companies like Dell or Wal-Mart have superior strategies and are successful *today* is no guarantee that they will be successful tomorrow. To be successful tomorrow, they will need to develop a strategy that will be superior in *tomorrow's* market; and to do that, they must understand the underlying principles of their successful strategy of today. Thus, even successful companies need to understand the logic of successful strategies. This is especially so if they arrived at their strategy by means of intuition, trial and error, or luck. It is highly unlikely that the same company will be "lucky" twice. But if its managers understand the principles of successful strategy making, they will be more likely to craft yet another superior strategy once their current strategy has run its course.

Structure of the Book

The basic premise of this book is that *superior strategy is all about finding and exploiting a unique strategic position in the company's business while at the same time searching for new strategic positions on a continuing basis.* From a managerial perspective, this raises several thorny issues, such as:

- What, exactly, is a strategic position and how can a company create a unique one in its business?

- How can an established company discover a new strategic position, especially at a time when its existing operations are quite profitable? How can an established company shift its attention away from improving its existing position to discovering a new one?

- How can a company know if a newly discovered position will turn out to be a profitable one?

• Even if a company discovers a new strategic position, can it manage two positions (the old and the new) at the same time? Is this even possible, or should the company focus on one of the two?

My aim in this book is to provide answers to these questions. After an introductory chapter, Part I (Chapters 2–7) explores the question "What is a strategic position and how can a company create a unique position in its industry?" Part II (Chapters 8–10) examines the consequences of introducing strategic innovation to the firm and explains how established companies can discover new strategic positions and then serve the old as well as the new at the same time—if that's the best course to take. Part II also explores the ways in which a company can phase out a strategy whose effectiveness is in decline while phasing in a new one to replace it.

While the ideas I present here are based on my research on a number of companies from a variety of countries and industries, I focus on a few instructive cases to highlight my points. In particular, I refer repeatedly to Edward Jones (Unites States), Nespresso (Switzerland), Lan & Spar Bank (Denmark), Canon (Japan), Boddington Group (United Kingdom), Hewitt Associates (United States), and Leclerc (France). These detailed case examples will be interspersed with material from several other companies as well as publicly available information.

Acknowledgments

I started writing this book three years ago. But the ideas in it first saw daylight as far back as 1990 and have matured and evolved over the years, aided by the contributions of the remarkable colleagues and senior executives with whom I have been privileged to work.

My first thanks go to my intellectual family at the London Business School and in particular to Sumantra Ghoshal and John Stopford. They have protected and nurtured me through the years, and in return I stole their ideas! Thank you.

A special thank you also to Booz·Allen & Hamilton and especially to Chuck Lucier and Bruce Pasternack for providing me and my colleagues in the strategy department of the London Business School with the financial resources to carry out our research. This book would not have been possible without their support. Thank you also to Harbir Singh and Ian MacMillan at Wharton, Orjan Solvell and Julian Birkinshaw at the Stockholm School of Economics, and Vassilis Papadakis at the Athens University of Economics and Business, all of whom provided me with an academic home during my sabbatical in 1996–97.

I am also grateful for the comments and advice of several other colleagues who read portions of this manuscript. Thank you to Harry Korine, Aya Chacar, Kim Warren, Don Sull, Dominic Houlder, Matthew Hayward, and Paul Geroski. I am particularly indebted to by brother Angelos, who tested many of the ideas in this book and gave me feedback on what worked and what didn't. My ideas have also benefited enormously from discussions and cooperative work with Peter Williamson, Gary Hamel, Paul Mang, Jose Santos, and Daniel Oyon. But above all, a special thank you to Costas Charitou. As my Ph.D. student over the past four years, he has been subjected to endless discussions on the subject of strategic innovation and has contributed enormously to the development of my ideas.

The ideas in this book derive from and have been test-run on several companies. A few of these companies and their executives prefer to remain anonymous. To all of them—you know who you are—thank you. I hope you recognize a part of yourselves in this book. A heartfelt thanks to Peter Schou at Lan & Spar and John Bachmann and Doug Hill at Edward Jones: your companies are the birthplace of most of the ideas in this book. Thank you also to Jean-Paul Gaillard at Nespresso, Denis Cassidy at Boddington, Dale Gifford and Jack Bruner at Hewitt Associates, Jacques van Dijk and Henk de Back at Douwe Egberts, Robert Davis at Schlumberger, Olof Stenhammar and Nils-Robert Persson at OM Group, Jean-Claude Biver at Blancpain, Peter Tillotson at Royal & SunAlliance, Graham Picken at First Direct, Pierre-Andre Steim at Migros, Peter Woods at Direct Line, Philip Twyman at CGU, and Haydan Leshel and Dr. Ulrich Hackenberg at Audi. Without your willingness to share your thoughts, it would have been impossible for me to write this book.

I have discussed most of the ideas in these pages with hundreds of executives around the globe. They have challenged me and helped me structure my thoughts in far better ways than I could have done on my own. I'd like to thank, in particular, executives at Honeywell, Warner Lambert, Pirelli, Gartmore, Bowthorpe, Novartis, Barings, Standard Chartered, Energizer, Tibbett & Britten, Unilever, Bass, Schroder, Hill & Knowlton, Rea Brothers, BP, Polygram, Abbey National, MAM, Threadneedle, and British Aerospace.

What you now hold in your hands is the fourth draft of this book. It has been a long and laborious journey, but throughout I have been fortunate to have the help, support, and insights of Marjorie Williams at the Harvard Business School Press. She has single-handedly shaped the structure and contents of this book. A special thanks to you Marjorie: without your help and guidance, this book would probably have been finished two years ago—but its quality is another matter! I am also grateful to the superb editorial assistance of Barbara Roth and India Koopman at HBS Press. I gave them an ugly duckling and they transformed it into a beautiful swan. A million thanks!

The only person who has read this manuscript from beginning to end in each of its four different drafts and has unfailingly provided comments and suggestions every time is my brother George. All this because I promised him a free copy when it was published! Here's to you George—you can have two free copies if you want.

London

1

Put Innovation Back into Strategy

The strategist's method is very simply to challenge the prevailing assumptions with a single question: why? and to put the same question relentlessly to those responsible for the current way of doing things until they are sick of it.

—Kenichi Ohmae, *The Mind of the Strategist: The Art of Japanese Business*

We've done some good work, but all of these products become obsolete so fast. . . . It will be some finite number of years, and I don't know the number—before our doom comes.

—Bill Gates, in *Daniel Gross, Forbes Greatest Business Stories of All Time*

In every industry, there are several viable positions that a company can occupy. The essence of strategy therefore is to choose the *one* position that your company will claim as its own. A strategic position is simply the sum of a company's answers to these three questions: *Who* should I target as customers? *What* products or services should I offer them? *How* should I do this?[1] Strategy is all about making tough choices in these three dimensions: the customers you will target and, just as important, the customers you will not target; the products or services you will offer and those you will not offer; and the activities you will engage in to sell your selected product to your selected customer and those you will not engage in. Ultimately, strategy is all about making choices, and a company will be successful if it chooses a *distinctive* strategic position—that is, a position different from that of each of its competitors. The most common source of strategic failure is the failure to make clear and explicit choices in each of these three dimensions.

Two Companies That Chose Wisely and Chose Well

The value of making smart choices along the who/what/how continuum is probably best shown by example. Here are the brief strategic histories of two companies that chose well.

The Case of Edward Jones

The St. Louis, Missouri–based partnership of Edward Jones, with 1996 capital of $465 million, is not the largest brokerage firm in the United States. In fact, it is only the thirty-fourth largest. But it is one of the most profitable in the volatile securities industry, and it's growing like wildfire. Since 1981, Edward Jones has expanded its broker force at an annual rate of 15 percent, without making any acquisitions. It now boasts more than 2,500 partners—up from a total of 8 in 1981.

As described by many outside observers, including Peter Drucker,[2] the firm is a federation of highly autonomous entrepreneurial units bound together by a strong set of values and beliefs. The entrepreneurial units are the brokers themselves, who operate out of one-person offices located in small communities all across America. They make their living by selling financial products to the people who live in those communities. Foremost among the values and beliefs these brokers have in common is this: their job is to offer sound, long-term financial advice to customers, even if that advice does not generate short-term fees for the brokers. The "customer-first" value is ingrained in every single broker working in the Jones system.

It wasn't always that way. During the past fifty years, the firm has gone through three evolutionary stages. It was originally set up by Edward Jones, Sr., as a financial department store—one-stop shopping to satisfy all of a customer's financial needs. In the 1960s the department store concept slowly evolved into a financial services delivery system for rural America. This change was due to Ted Jones, son of Mr. Jones, Sr., who grew the firm into a network of 200 offices across the country. No longer traveling salesmen who passed through town every week or two, the brokers became more a part of the community. The idea was to convert Edward Jones into a distribution network to sell mutual funds in rural America.

The third stage in the evolution of Edward Jones began in 1970, after the arrival of John Bachmann, who is today the firm's managing partner. In what he describes as a "defining moment" for the firm, Bachmann set about to convert Jones into a "merchant"— that is, an informed buyer for the end-customer. According to Bachmann, the difference between being a distributor and being a merchant is crucial:

> A distributor is structured around the product and tries to sell only profitable products. A merchant, on the other hand, is structured around the end-consumer. He acts as an informed buyer for the investor, selecting only the products that are good for the investor, as opposed to products that generate fees for the brokers. Most investment firms look at brokers as their customers. We don't. For us, the customer is the individual investor that signs the checks.

This vision of being a merchant for the individual investor has guided the company's every move since 1980. It has also shaped its current successful strategy, the main elements of which are the following:

- Unlike its major competitors (Merrill Lynch and Smith Barney, for instance), which sell their own in-house mutual funds, Edward Jones does not manufacture the products it sells. Instead, it acts as a distributor for the products of a few selected manufacturers, such as Capital Research, Putnam, and Morgan Stanley.

- Unlike most of its competitors, the company targets and sells its products only to individual investors, never to institutional investors.

- The firm sets up offices in selected areas, usually small towns or specific areas within cities where there is a "sense of community." In nearly all cases—and contrary to traditional wisdom, which favors the exploitation of economies of scale—the Jones office is a one-person operation. That person has extraordinary autonomy, managing the office as if it were his or her own business. Every branch is a profit center. Brokers are tied to the home office through a satellite communications network that broadcasts homemade TV programming.

- The firm sells only selected products—often transparent, long-term products such as large-cap equities and highly rated bonds. It avoids selling risky initial public offerings, options, and commodity futures.

- The firm remains a partnership so that people feel and think like owners, not employees.

- The glue that binds everything together is the company culture: everyone behaves like a member of a family whose mission is to help ordinary people invest their money wisely.

The company has obviously made explicit choices as to who to target, what to sell, and how to do this (see Exhibit 1-1). Bachmann likes to point out that the adoption of every one of these important components of the company's very successful strategy involved some kind of trade-off:

> We target individual investors, not institutional ones. We buy good securities and keep them a long time instead of trying to maximize transaction fees. Rather than have big offices in large cities, our offices are small and are placed in small communities to be convenient to the customer. Our offices are one-person operations. . . . We do not manufacture our products, and we showcase the products of a limited number of leading houses. We do not sell all products—we select transparent and safe products to promote. We remain a partnership rather than try to go public.

These choices were not easy to make. But they were made. And the company has remained faithful to them for more than twenty years. As Bachmann says, "These principles are cast in stone. We don't debate these things."

The Case of Nespresso

Another example of a company that has built its success on developing and exploiting a unique strategic position is the Nestlé subsidiary Nespresso. Nespresso represents one of the most innovative products developed by Swiss giant Nestlé. The product is basically a system that allows the consumer to produce a fresh cup

---

Exhibit 1-1   Strategic Choices Made at Edward Jones

The Who	"Who should I target as customers?"	• Target individual investors rather than institutional investors. • Target individuals who live in areas where "there is a sense of community."
The What	"What products or services should I offer?"	• Offer transparent, long-term products such as large-cap equities and highly rated bonds. Never sell risky initial public offerings or commodity futures.
The How	"How can I best deliver these services to these customers?"	• Never manufacture my own products—act only as distributor. • Buy only from a few reputable suppliers (such as Capital Research and Morgan Stanley). • Operate as one-person offices located in the community. • Remain a partnership. • Focus on the end-customer, not the broker.

---

of espresso coffee at home. Though simple in appearance and use, Nestlé spent more than ten years developing it.

The system consists of two parts: a coffee capsule and a machine. The coffee capsule is hermetically sealed in aluminum and contains 5 grams (about one teaspoon) of roasted and ground coffee. The machine has four parts—a handle, a water container, a pump, and an electrical heating system.

The use of the Nespresso system is straightforward. The coffee capsule is placed in the handle, which is then inserted into the body of the machine. The act of inserting the handle into the machine pierces the coffee capsule at the top. At the press of a button, pressurized, steamed water is passed through the capsule. The result is a creamy, foamy, high-quality cup of espresso coffee.

Nespresso was introduced in 1986, and the strategy behind it was the following. Nestlé was to set up a joint venture between Nespresso and a Swiss-based distributor called Sobal. The new venture, Sobal-Nespresso, was to purchase the coffee-making machines from another Swiss company, Turmix, and the coffee capsules from Nestlé. Sobal-Nespresso would then distribute and sell everything as a system—one product, one price. Offices and restaurants were targeted as the customers, and a separate unit, called Nespresso S.A., was set up within Nestlé to support the joint venture's sales and marketing efforts and to service and maintain the machines.

By 1988, the whole thing was an acknowledged nonstarter, and headquarters was considering freezing the operation. That's when Jean-Paul Gaillard arrived on the scene, first as commercial director of Nespresso S.A. and then as CEO of Nestlé Coffee Specialties S.A.—the new name for the former Nespresso S.A. unit. The strategy he introduced in 1988–89 turned the operation around and established the unit as a profitable and growing enterprise within Nestlé.

Gaillard introduced several changes, but the logic that drove all his actions was the belief that the coffee side of the operation had to be separated from the machine side. Since Nestlé was not in the machine business, he felt he had to focus on coffee.

On the machine side, he assigned the manufacture of the Nespresso machine to a Swiss-based original equipment manufacturer, which then supplied a variety of carefully selected manufacturers, such as Krups, National, Turmix, and Philips. These companies, in turn, sold the Nespresso machine to prestigious retailers such as Harrods, Galeries Lafayette, and Bloomingdale's. It was the responsibility of these retailers—under the guidance and control of Nespresso—to promote, demonstrate, and finally sell the machine to the end-consumer. It was also the responsibility of the machine partners—such as Krups, National, and Philips—to service and maintain the machines.

On the coffee side, the Sobal partnership was terminated and the whole operation placed under Nespresso S.A. (later Nestlé Coffee

Specialties S.A.). The target customer was changed from offices to households and the distribution of coffee capsules was organized through a "club." Once a customer bought a machine, he or she became a member of the Nespresso Club. Orders of capsules were made over the phone or by fax direct to the club, and the capsules were shipped to the customer's home within twenty-four hours. The club currently takes 7,000 orders per day.

The company has ambitious plans for the future. Prominent among these is the creation of two new products to target two new customer segments: small offices and young Internet users. Eventually, the objective is to have a Nespresso machine in every kitchen in the world. (See Exhibit 1-2 for a description of Nestlé's strategic choices in terms of "who," "what," and "how.")

Exhibit 1-2   Strategic Choices Made at Nespresso

The Who	"Who should I target as customers?"	• Target individuals and households, *not* restaurants or offices.
The What	"What products or services should I offer?"	• Sell coffee, *not* coffee machines. • Educate retailers so that they can teach the end-consumer how to use the machine.
The How	"How can I best deliver this product to these customers?"	• Subcontract the manufacture of the Nespresso machine to a prestigious OEM. • Focus on the manufacture of high-quality coffee capsules. • Sell the Nespresso machine through prestigious retailers, such as Harrods, Galeries Lafayette, and Bloomingdale's. • Sell the coffee capsules direct through the "Nespresso Club."

As was the case with Edward Jones, Nespresso has made clear and explicit choices concerning who to target, what to sell, and how to do this. It turns out that the original choices made did not produce the desired results. However, the new choices made by Jean-Paul Gaillard in 1988–89 have rejuvenated Nespresso and turned it into a profitable unit within Nestlé.

Unfortunately, No Position Remains Unique Forever

Nespresso and Edward Jones built their success on finding and exploiting unique strategic positions in their industries. They did not try to imitate the strategic positions of their competitors. Nor did they try to do their competitors one better by competing with them directly. Instead, these companies created unique positions for themselves that allowed them to play entirely different games. Of course, no position can be totally different from all others, but the idea is to create as much differentiation as possible.

There is no question that *success stems from the exploitation of a unique strategic position*. Unfortunately, no position can remain unique or attractive forever. The firm lucky enough to be in one will be imitated by aggressive competitors, and, perhaps more important, supplanted by even more aggressive competitors, those which develop new strategic positions in the market.

New strategic positions keep emerging all the time. A new strategic position is simply a new viable who/what/how combination—perhaps a new customer segment (a new *who*), a new value proposition (a new *what*), or a new way of distributing or manufacturing a product (a new *how*). Over time, the players with the new positions will rise to challenge the status quo—the firms that have grown too comfortable in what once were their unique positions.

This cycle occurs in one industry after another. Once-formidable companies that built their success on what seemed to be unassailable strategic positions find themselves humbled by relative unknowns that base their attacks on creating and exploiting new strategic positions in the industry. The rise and fall of Xerox in the period 1960–90 exemplifies this simple but powerful point.

In the 1960s, Xerox put a lock on the copier market by deploying a well-defined and successful strategy. The main elements of this strategy were as follows. Having segmented the market by volume, Xerox decided to go after the corporate reproduction market by concentrating on copiers designed for high-speed, high-volume needs. This inevitably defined Xerox's customers as big corporations, which in turn determined its distribution method: the direct sales force. At the same time, Xerox decided to lease rather than sell its machines, a strategic choice that had worked well in the company's earlier battles with 3M.

The Xerox strategy was clear and precise, with sharp boundaries. Critical choices were made as to who to target (big corporations), what product features to emphasize (high speed), and how to deliver them (direct sales force and leasing). These were not easy choices, and there were no doubt lively debates and disagreements within Xerox about whether these decisions were the correct ones. Yet, at the end of the day, hard choices were made. And, at the time, they were good ones. Xerox prospered because it developed a distinctive strategic position in its industry, based on a well-defined customer base, well-defined products, and a well-defined system of delivering those products to those customers. Throughout the 1960s and early 1970s, Xerox maintained a return on equity (ROE) of around 20 percent.

Xerox's strategy proved to be so successful that several new competitors, among them IBM and Kodak, tried to enter this huge market, essentially by adopting the same or similar strategies. Fundamentally, their strategy was to grab market share by being *better* than Xerox—by offering better products or better service at lower prices. For example, IBM entered the market in 1970 with its first model, the IBM Copier I, which was clearly aimed at the medium- and high-volume segments and was marketed by IBM's sales force on a rental basis. Similarly, Kodak entered the market in 1975 with the Ektaprint 100 copier/duplicator, also aimed at the high-volume end of the market and sold as a high-quality, low-price substitute for the Xerox machines.

Neither of these corporate giants managed to make substantial inroads in the copier business. While there are many possible reasons for their failure, one was undoubtedly their inability to create a distinctive position for themselves. Instead, they tried to "colonize" Xerox's position. Given the first-mover advantages that Xerox enjoyed in its own strategic position, it is no surprise that IBM and Kodak failed.

Canon, on the other hand, chose to play the game differently. Having determined in the early 1960s to diversify from cameras into copiers, Canon decided to segment the market by end-user, targeting small and medium-sized businesses while also producing PC copiers for the individual. At the same time, Canon decided to sell its machines through a dealer network rather than lease them. And while Xerox emphasized the speed of its machines, Canon elected to focus on quality and price as differentiating features. To get to the end of the story, whereas IBM's and Kodak's assaults on the copier market failed, Canon's succeeded. Within twenty years of entering the market, Canon emerged as the leader, not only in the new territory it had at first staked out for itself but also on Xerox's turf.

Again, there are many reasons behind Canon's success. Notice, however, that just as Xerox had done twenty years before, Canon also created for itself a distinctive strategic position in the industry. Whereas Xerox targeted big corporations as its customers, Canon went after small companies and individuals; while Xerox emphasized the speed of its machines, Canon accentuated quality and price; and whereas Xerox employed a direct sales force to lease its machines, Canon used its dealer network to sell its copiers. Instead of trying to beat Xerox at its own game, Canon ultimately triumphed (as explained below) by creating its own unique strategic position. (See Exhibit 1-3 for a summary of Xerox's and Canon's strategies.)

Exhibit 1-3   Xerox versus Canon: A Case of Different Strategies

Strategy Component	Xerox	Canon
Product	Plain paper copiers (PPCs)	Start with coated paper copiers (CPCs) and then move to PPCs
Copier volume	High	Low → High
Targeted customers	Big corporations	End-users
Method of selling	Lease	Sell
Distribution	Sales force	Dealer network
Differentiating features	Speed	Quality and price

New Positions Emerge All the Time

The kind of campaign that Canon launched against Xerox is actually very common. All around us, in industry after industry, companies rise to fame and fortune only to see their once formidable positions become susceptible to attack as new players enter the field from newly created strategic positions. Take a look at Exhibit 1-4.

All the companies in the column labeled "Dominant Competitors" built their success on unique strategic positions that they created for themselves in their respective industries. Over time, their positions have been imitated by the competitors in the "Traditional Competitors" column. And all of these companies—dominant and traditional competitor alike—are now fighting it out for market share. But the real winners in each market are those companies which launch their attacks from newly created positions—the "Strategic Innovators" in each industry. While the established competitors are battling one another for marginal gains in the same share of the market, the strategic innovators are running away with huge chunks of the market—often, a *new* market that they themselves helped create.

Komatsu, for example, increased its market share in the earthmoving equipment business from 10 percent to 25 percent in just under fifteen years. Canon went from zero to 35 percent market share in the copier business in little more than twenty years. *USA Today* was launched in 1982 and by 1993 had become the top-selling newspaper in the country, with sales of more than 5 million copies a day. Dell emerged from its college-dorm beginnings in the mid-1980s to capture more than 10 percent of the global personal computer market in fewer than ten years. First Direct was launched in 1989 as the United Kingdom's first dedicated telephone bank, and within seven years was boasting nearly 700,000 customers—a feat that the business press described as "a miraculous cure" for the stagnant U.K. banking industry.[3] Starbucks Coffee grew from a chain of 11 stores and sales of $1.3 million in 1987 to 280 stores and sales of $163.5 million in just five years (and it now boasts more than 2,000 stores). Direct Line was started in 1985, and within ten years became one of Britain's biggest automobile insurers, with 2.2 million policy holders.

Exhibit 1-4 New Strategic Positions Undermine the Established Ones

Industry	Dominant Competitors	Traditional Competitors	Strategic Innovators
Airlines	American Airlines	Delta Northwest United	Southwest Airlines
Car rentals	Hertz	Avis Europcar National	Enterprise Rent-A-Car
Coffee	General Foods (Maxwell House)	Nestlé (Nescafe) Procter & Gamble (Folgers) Sara Lee (Douwe Egberts)	Starbucks
Earth-moving equipment	Caterpillar	International Harvester J. I. Case John Deere	Komatsu
Newspapers	*Chicago Tribune* *New York Times* *Washington Post*	Other regional newspapers	*USA Today*
Personal computers	IBM	Compaq Hewlett-Packard NEC Packard Bell Toshiba	Dell
Photocopiers	Xerox	IBM Kodak Nicoh	Canon
Securities	Merrill Lynch	Dean Witter PaineWebber Smith Barney	Edward Jones
Steel	U.S. Steel	Bethlehem Inland National	Nucor
TV broadcasting	NBC	ABC CBS	CNN
U.K. airlines	British Airways	British Midlands Other European carriers Virgin Atlantic	easyJet
U.K. banking	Natwest	Barclays Lloyds	First Direct
U.K. insurance	Norwich Union	Prudential Royal Sun Alliance	Direct Line

All of these companies became successful not by trying to beat the establishment at its own game but by breaking the rules of the game—that is, creating for themselves strategic positions that were completely different from those occupied by established competitors. The common element in all of these successful attacks is strategic innovation: the creation of new and distinct strategic positions.

Companies Must Search for New Positions Continually

New strategic positions—that is, new combinations of who/ what/how—are emerging all the time. Changing industry conditions, changing customer needs or preferences, moves and countermoves by competitors, and a company's own evolving competencies give rise to new opportunities and new ways of playing the game. Unless a company continually questions its accepted norms and behaviors, it will never know that other options have emerged. More agile players will jump in and take the lead.

A company must therefore never settle for what it has. While fighting it out in its current position, it must continually search for new positions to colonize. As simple and obvious as this may sound, it contrasts sharply with the way most companies compete in their industries. Most firms take their current position and the established rules of the game as givens and pour their energy into *bettering* each other at that same old game—usually through such practices as restructuring, process reengineering, quality control, or cost and differentiation strategies. Few actually try to figure out how to make themselves *different* from one another. (See Exhibit 1-5.) Evidence of this can be seen in the fact that most companies that strategically innovate by breaking the rules of the game are small niche players or new market entrants. It is rare to find a strategic innovator that is also a big, established industry player—a fact that suggests just how hard it is to risk the sure thing for an uncertain outcome.

Consider, for example, the way Xerox responded to the Canon challenge. Its initial response was to ignore the threat posed by Canon. After all, Canon was targeting a different customer segment—not to mention the fact that this segment was a small niche in a huge market so was of little interest to Xerox. Writing in the

---

Exhibit 1-5   Being Better versus Being Different

Playing the Game Better

- Focus on your existing strategic position

- Try to improve that position

- To accomplish this, engage in practices such as restructuring, refocusing, process reengineering, quality programs, employee empowerment, and the like

Playing the Game Differently

- Try to identify new or unexploited customer segments to focus on (a new *who*)

- Try to identify new customer needs that no competitor is currently satisfying (a new *what*)

- Try to identify new ways of producing, delivering, selling, or distributing your products or services (a new *how*)

To be successful, a company must be able to do *both!*

---

early 1990s, Xerox's corporate vice president, John Seely Brown, admitted that the company was slow to react because it underestimated the potential of this newly created market niche: "We had been late to recognize market opportunities for low- and mid-range copiers and Japanese competitors like Canon were cutting into our market share."[4] It is also important to acknowledge that if Xerox had responded to Canon by trying to imitate Canon's strategic position, its own unique position would have suffered—for example, how would Xerox's salespeople feel if Xerox had suddenly adopted a dealer network? For a variety of reasons, then, Xerox did not respond to Canon at first.

What did Xerox do? Conscious of the strength of its own position, it sought to achieve growth by building on that position in two ways: (1) by taking its distinctive strategy international, basically replicating in other geographic markets the game plan that had worked for it in the United States; and (2) by making its position still more attractive, so as to lure customers away from other competitors. Xerox improved product quality, cut costs, added new features, and tried to communicate its superiority to customers through heavy advertising. In the meantime, Canon was applying very similar thinking to its own unique position, taking it international and trying to make it more attractive so that it could convert Xerox customers to its own proposition.

Under normal circumstances, the Xerox strategy should have worked very well. Rather than blurring its unique position by imitating Canon, Xerox correctly focused its efforts on optimizing its own strengths. Unfortunately for Xerox, however, the small and uninteresting niche that Canon had targeted—the individual and the small to medium-sized business—simply exploded in the 1970s. By the early 1980s, it had become as big as the corporate market.

At the same time, Canon was slowly "invading" Xerox's position by beginning to target big corporations with high-speed, high-quality photocopiers. When Canon entered the high-volume segment in 1978 with the NP8500, for example, it was clearly going after the market for the Xerox 9200. In addition, Canon was broadening its distribution channels to include not only dealers but also a strong direct sales force and independent sales subsidiaries. Canon was thus doing what Xerox had been so reluctant to do: occupying two different strategic positions at the same time. Given this turn of events, Xerox could no longer afford to ignore Canon's strategic position.

In early 1980, Xerox decided to go after Canon wholeheartedly. It introduced new products, especially at the low-volume end, and restructured sales operations to create dedicated organizations for large system customers and small businesses. In addition, Xerox opened retail stores that sold small copiers (as well as other products). The company renewed its emphasis on cutting costs, improving product quality, adding features to the copiers, and achieving better coordination and integration between subsidiaries.

The strategy amounted to a frontal attack on Canon. Since Canon had already encroached on Xerox's strategic position, the outcome of the Xerox attack was to create a situation in which both competitors occupied two strategic positions simultaneously: their own and each other's. In a sense, their strategies had become identical, which made it extremely difficult for customers to decide between the two. Since both competitors were now targeting the same customers with roughly similar products, the only way for either one to gain any advantage was to try to become *better* than the other—primarily through cost or differentiation strategies. Needless to say, this type of competition is destructive and eventually leads to price deterioration. As expected, profit margins in the business declined sharply in the 1980s. Xerox's return on equity declined from 20 percent in the early 1970s to 6 to 8 percent in the mid-1980s. Similarly, return on sales for both Xerox and Canon dropped from around 6 percent in the early 1980s to less than 3 percent by the end of the 1980s.

Xerox's response (and its unfortunate outcome) should not come as a surprise. Most established companies forget that what made them successful was a decision made a long time ago to create a new and unique strategic position. Over time, they become entrenched in their strategic position. Believing that all possible positions have already been colonized by competitors, *they shift their attention to protecting and improving their current positions. Little attention is paid to searching for or discovering new strategic positions in the industry.* Yet this is exactly what is required—a continual search for new sources of advantage and new ways of playing the game.

This is a point that has not escaped the attention of Xerox and Canon. By the early 1990s, both companies were looking for ways to "rejuvenate" the copier business. Intense rivalry had sliced Canon's margins to a wafer-thin 1.8 percent in 1992, while Xerox had gone $1 billion into the red that same year. In addition, managers at both companies were haunted by the fear that another, perhaps unknown competitor might appear and break what had now become the established rules of the game. Better to be the first to discover a new position.

Canon is certainly thinking in this way. According to a report in *Fortune* magazine in early 1998, "Canon's headquarters today feels like a restless, uncertain place. There is a gnawing anxiety that Canon needs to branch out into some new category of technology. The fear is that some of Canon's current products could go the way of the electric typewriter." The same writer continued, "Canon has adopted a two-pronged strategy. It will maintain profits in its core business by cutting costs, making its suppliers more efficient and speeding up its product development. At the same time, Canon needs to move into the digital age. To do this, it plans to cultivate alliances with companies that know the networking and computer world better than Canon."[5]

Canon is searching for a new strategic position in the copier business or even for a totally different business. It is impossible at this point to tell whether that search will be successful. But clearly Canon has recognized that trying to improve its current position is not enough—it must find and colonize a new position. The same applies to Xerox.

Established Companies Make Lousy Innovators

In industry after industry, leading companies are becoming masters at playing the performance improvement game and are having little difficulty stymieing competitors who play by the same rules. Yet it seems that the better they play their chosen game, the harder it is for them to conceive of or play a different one and the more easily they fall victim to an upstart who attacks by changing the rules.

Thus, Xerox had little trouble protecting its position against fierce competitors like IBM and Kodak, yet lost out to Canon, a little-known camera manufacturer from Japan. Caterpillar Tractor Co. met the challenges of well-known competitors such as International Harvester, John Deere, and J. I. Case, yet lost significant ground to another relatively unknown Japanese company, Komatsu. Broadcaster CBS was able to stand up to ABC and NBC, yet was outflanked by a start-up, CNN. While Natwest Bank in the United Kingdom competed effectively against its major competitors, Barclays and Lloyds, it was virtually defenseless against the tactics of the new kid on the block, First Direct. Hertz seems to have little trouble slugging it out with huge competitors like Avis and National, yet it is losing ground to a newcomer—Enterprise. American Airlines is able to stand its ground against fierce global competitors such as British Airways and United, but seems to have no rebuff for Southwest Airlines.

There are many reasons why established companies have difficulty becoming strategic innovators (see Exhibit 1-6). Compared with new entrants or niche players, leaders are weighed down by *structural* and *cultural* inertia, internal politics, complacency, fear of

---

Exhibit 1-6   Obstacles to Strategic Innovation

- **Why change or risk what I have?**
  I already have an established strategic position that is keeping the company profitable and growing. Why search for anything else, especially if the new strategic position I discover cannibalizes my existing position?

- **Change into what?**
  Even if I wanted to carve out a new strategic position, I wouldn't know what it should be. We are all "blinded" by our own strong mental models and sacred cows. How can we learn to see past them?

- **Will it be a winner?**
  Even if I see a new strategic position out there, how will I know if it will grow and become a winner? What if I jump into it and it fails?

- **Can I do both?**
  Even if I decide to jump into a new strategic position, how can I make sure that my employees (who have vested interests in maintaining the status quo) jump with me? Can I manage two strategic positions simultaneously, or do I have to give up the old for the new? And if I can have both positions, how do I organize to manage the old and the new simultaneously?

---

cannibalizing existing products, fear of destroying existing competencies, satisfaction with the status quo, and a general lack of incentive to abandon a certain present for an uncertain future. In addition, because there are fewer industry leaders than potential new entrants, the chances that an innovator will emerge from the ranks of the leaders are undeniably small.

Nothing Ventured, Nothing Gained

Given all these barriers to innovation, it is understandable why we do not see more strategic innovators emerging from the ranks of established industry players. Yet we are not without examples. Consider the following two:

Kresge/Kmart: In 1959, when Harry Cunningham became president of Kresge, the company (which was originally founded in 1897) was second only to Woolworth among U.S. variety store chains. In the next few years, Cunningham transformed Kresge from a variety retailer into the largest discount store in the United States—what we now know as Kmart. The decision to go into discounting was a particularly difficult one, because, as Cunningham explained, "Discounting at the time had a terrible odor. . . . If I had announced my intentions ahead of time, I never would have made president. . . . I had the authority, but if you haven't sold the people in your organization, you'll fall flat on your face. I had to convince them that they were an important part of an exciting venture."[6] The move into discounting rejuvenated the company. By 1976, Kmart was doing almost twice the sales volume of Woolworth and was second only to Sears among general merchandise retailers.

Schwab: In 1995, the low-cost brokerage firm Schwab had no Internet business to speak of. Three years later, more than half the company's total trading volume is carried out on Schwab's Web site, and about one-third of its total customer assets come from customers who are active on-line investors.[7] Started as a separate internal venture, Schwab's electronic unit was quickly integrated into the rest of the organization so that customers could purchase the same product at the same price, no matter what distribution method they used (phone, branch office, or Internet). Schwab began by offering two separate concepts to the customer (to avoid excessive cannibalization) but quickly merged the two in response to customer demands.

These stories are more than successful examples of corporate turnaround or inspired stories of dramatic improvements in the existing business, and they are more than successful internal venturing decisions or successful attempts to add another business to the existing product portfolio. They are all examples of *strategic innovation*—that is, a fundamental reconceptualization of what the business is about, which in turn leads to a dramatically *different* way of playing the game in the industry.

What can we learn from the experiences of these firms? Simple: Strategic innovation is not the birthright of small companies alone. Established competitors and industry leaders can and should engage in strategic innovation as well. Granted, compared with new entrants or new start-ups, established companies face some formidable obstacles (as mentioned above). But in the long run, established companies cannot afford *not* to attempt strategic innovation. If they don't, someone else surely will.

The fact that several established competitors have been able to do it should give hope to others that may want to try. Consider, for example, the rejuvenation of Intel in 1984–85. Up to that time, Intel engaged primarily in the production of DRAMs (dynamic random access memory products). Intel introduced DRAMs in 1970, and these products replaced magnetic core memory as the standard technology for storing instructions and data on computers. Intel based its success in the period 1970–80 on the success of these products.

By the early 1980s, however, cheap Japanese products were beginning to take market share from Intel. The DRAMs business was turned into a commodity business, and the Japanese were winning the price wars. Using their large-scale precision manufacturing skills to obtain high yields, they outcompeted Intel. After a long and politically charged process of soul searching, Intel decided in 1984–85 to exit the DRAMs business and focus on microprocessors. In so doing, Intel transformed itself from a memory company into a microprocessor company. The decision was so drastic and painful that one senior Intel manager described it as follows: "It was kind of like Ford getting out of cars."[8]

Today, Intel is facing another challenge: the emergence of a new market for cheap microprocessors. The new market consists of consumer electronics such as smart identification cards, Internet-ready telephones, handheld computers, digital cameras, advanced video-game players, and other non-PC devices. These new products run not on advanced and expensive microprocessors but on cheap ones. Intel chips are too expensive for this market; the company is losing it to competitors such as LSI Logic and Silicon Graphics. The big issue for Intel is this: Its own major market (the PC market) is $160 billion big and growing at 15 percent per year. Can Intel continue to focus on this market while at the same time develop a strategy to build low-cost, high-performance chips for the non-PC market? Can it play both games at once? Estimates suggest that unit shipments of non-PC devices will exceed consumer PC shipments by the year 2002. Can Intel afford to overlook this market?

Polaroid is facing a similar challenge. Digital imaging has emerged as a major new strategic position in the photography business, and Polaroid must decide how to exploit it. According to its CEO, Gary DiCamillo, "Some people think photography is going to go away as everything in our industry becomes digitized. But I disagree. I think analog photography will endure, because it still satisfies many users, and digital imaging businesses will grow up around it, creating a much bigger, faster-growing market. Our challenge will be deciding which of those markets to pursue."[9]

The mindset that established players must develop is that *strategies are not cast in concrete*. A company needs to remain flexible and ready to adjust its strategy if the feedback from the market is not favorable. Equally important, a company needs to continually question its current mode of operations in constant search of new strategic positions.

The continual questioning of one's established strategic position serves two vital purposes. First, it allows a company to identify the deterioration of that position early on.[10] Second, and more important, it gives the company the opportunity to proactively explore the emerging terrain, situating itself to be the first to discover the new and attractive strategic positions waiting to be exploited. If Xerox had kept questioning its existing (profitable) position, perhaps it would have identified and exploited the new strategic position that Canon ended up colonizing. Who knows?

This is no guarantee of success, of course. Questioning one's established strategies will not automatically lead to untapped strategic gold mines. But the possibility—even a remote one—of discovering something new will *never* arise if these questions go unasked.

Summary

1. A company will succeed if it develops a strategy that allows it to create and colonize a unique strategic position in its industry. (Consider Edward Jones, Nespresso, and Canon.)

2. No position will remain unique forever. Aggressive competitors not only imitate attractive positions, they create new ones, and these can pose a much greater threat. Over time, these new positions can grow to challenge the attractiveness of the dominant positions of the day. (Consider the success of Komatsu over Caterpillar and of Nucor over U.S. Steel.)

3. Because no position remains unique forever, established competitors must continually strive to discover new strategic positions in their business. If they don't do it, somebody else will. (Consider Canon and Xerox.)

4. Unfortunately, most established competitors are not good at seeking, let alone actually discovering, such new positions. Even though their success today can be traced back to an earlier decision to create a unique strategic position for themselves, they now expend little energy on such efforts. Instead, they spend most of their time trying to improve the position they already have.

5. The bottom line: Improving one's current position is not enough. A company that succeeded by creating a unique position for itself twenty or thirty years ago must do that again and again if it is to succeed into the future.

PART I

How to Create a Unique Strategic Position

To be successful, a company must create and exploit a unique strategic position in its industry. This essentially means that a company must do three things:

1. Define what business it believes it is in.

2. Decide *who* will be its targeted customers, *what* products or services it will offer them, and *how* it will achieve all this in an efficient way.

3. Construct the appropriate organizational environment that will support the choices made.

The first ingredient of a superior strategic position is the explicit answer to the question, "What business are we in?" Although very few companies actually ask themselves this question, let alone answer it, my research suggests that this is the single, most important step in the crafting of a superior strategy. Why? Because a company's implicit or explicit perception of the business it is in conditions everything that company "sees" and "does." The definition of the business is the filter through which all information passes. It is the filter that tells managers which opportunities to pursue and which to reject as "not applicable to our business." Thus, what business a company believes it is in conditions who it sees as its customers and its competitors and what it sees as its competitive advantage. It also determines what are thought to be the keys to success in the business and thus ultimately determines how it is going to play the game—that is, plan and execute its strategy. Given the important role that this "filter" plays in the development of strategy, it is only appropriate that managers give it considerable thought.

The second ingredient of a superior strategic position resides in finding answers to the questions who, what, and how. Who should we target as customers? What products and services should we offer them? How should we do this in an efficient way?

The questions of "who" and the "what" are essentially strategic; the answers to these questions will define the game the company will play. And this must be decided only after careful consideration of the underlying economics of the business and the company's competences. It should not be made ad hoc.

The question of "how" is also strategic—as most managers perceive it to be. What they may not perceive, however, is that it is next to impossible to decide on "how" without first answering the questions of "who" and "what." Deciding on "how" involves making choices on numerous issues, such as how to configure the value chain, what technology to adopt, what activities to handle in-house and what to subcontract, what specific functional policies (purchasing, manufacturing, marketing, accounting, and so on) to adopt, how to organize internally, and so on. Although these decisions are obviously important ones, strategy is much more than this! Strategy is all about *combining* these activities into a *system* that creates the requisite *fit* between what the environment needs and what the company does. Thus, it is not just the development of individual strategic activities that is important, but also the combination of these activities into a reinforcing system.

The third and final ingredient of a superior strategic position is to develop the necessary competencies and the appropriate organizational environment (or context) that will support the choices made. By organizational environment, I mean four basic things: the organization's culture, its incentives, its structure, and its people.

This means that to create a superior strategy, a company must think beyond markets, products, and customers. It must also decide what competencies to develop and what organizational context to create so as to facilitate the implementation of its strategy. But even after deciding on competencies or culture, structure, and incentives, the firm is still not done with strategy. As in the case of deciding on "how," the real challenge is to develop the individual pieces and then put them together in such a way that they support and complement each other on one hand while they collectively support and promote the chosen strategy on the other. The task is not only to create the appropriate individual parts of the system but to put them together in such a way as to create a strong and reinforcing system.

The next six chapters explore these issues in more detail: Chapter 2 examines the first ingredient of a superior strategic position—the appropriate definition of the business. Chapter 3 examines the questions of "who" and "what," while Chapter 4 explores the question of "how." The next two chapters examine the third ingredient of a superior strategic position: Chapter 5 discusses the means through which a firm can accumulate the skills and assets required to support its activities, while Chapter 6 examines the ways in which a firm can build the organizational context to support the choices it has made on the who/what/how continuum. Chapter 7 explores the process through which all these strategic decisions are made.

2

Decide What
Your Business Is

The railroads are in trouble today . . . because they assumed themselves to be in the railroad business rather than in the transportation
business. The reason they defined their industry wrong was because
they were railroad-oriented instead of transportation-oriented; they
were product-oriented instead of customer-oriented.

—Theodore Levitt, "Marketing Myopia"

I recently tried the following exercise with my students at London
Business School. I asked them to split into pairs and to arm-wrestle
for thirty seconds. I told them that the winner would be the one
who managed to push his or her opponent's hand down the greatest number of times in the allotted time. After some initial hesita-
tion, they all got down to it and for thirty seconds the room was
filled with laughter as the students tried to beat out their opponents.

At the end of the exercise, I went around the room and asked
each student to tell me how many times they had been successful.
Most replied two or three times. But a couple of students said a
hundred times. This was greeted with loud laughter, as most students asked: "How is it possible to push your opponent's hand
down one hundred times in just thirty seconds?" The students' assumption was that these two must have made a mistake. But there
was no mistake. When asked how they did it, the two students explained that instead of competing, they had chosen to cooperate
by offering no resistance to each other's pushing.

These students were the winners because they adopted a strategy
of cooperation while everyone else was trying to compete their way
toward the objective. The lesson here is not that cooperation always wins out over competition. That result is just a function of

this particular game. Rather, the point is that so many of the participants overlooked such an "obvious" solution to the problem. The
notion that they could cooperate to achieve their objective never
even crossed their minds.[1] What can explain such a phenomenon?
What is it that often seems to make people overlook the obvious?

Managing Mental Models

What makes us think "in a box" and miss the obvious is our
mental models of how the world should work. A mental model is
nothing more than a belief about any issue—whether it involves
our family or our business or the world as a whole. Thus, when
someone says, "I think everybody should go to church on Sunday,"
that person is simply expressing his or her mental model of the
subject—that is, whether going to church is good or bad. The term
mental model occurs in business literature under many guises. A recent survey of the academic literature alone identified eighty-one
words—such as *managerial frames, mindsets, sacred cows, blind spots,
paradigms, assumptions, templates, cognitive maps, managerial lenses,*
and so on (see Exhibit 2-1)—that have been used to describe the
same thing.[2]

As individuals, we develop mental models over time, primarily
through education and experience. Similarly, organizations develop mental models that are manifested in their culture, routines,
and unwritten rules of behavior. Thus, we hear statements such as
"This is how we do business in this industry" or "We never cut the
price of our products," which are nothing more than the expres-
sion of that organization's mental models. Organizational mental
models are also developed over time, primarily through company
training programs, word of mouth, and experience.

What makes mental models interesting is their ability to shape
our behavior. They do this by acting as "filters" through which all
incoming information passes. Whatever we "see" or "hear" passes
through these filters. Since we all have different filters, it is not unusual for two people to hear the same thing or see the same picture
and yet interpret what they've heard or seen differently. Since it is
the interpretation of the data that leads to behavior, people will behave differently even if they share the "same" information.

Exhibit 2-1   Another Way of Saying "Mental Model"

- Managerial perceptions
- Blinkered perceptions
- Cognitive maps
- Interpretive schemes
- Implicit theories
- Screens
- Frames
- Templates
- Causal maps
- Core causal beliefs
- Industry recipes
- Perception filters
- Belief structures
- Strategic myopia
- Tacit understanding

- Mindscapes
- Worldview
- Sacred cows
- Managerial lenses
- Assumptions
- Mental pictures
- Organizing frameworks
- Strategic frames
- Construed reality
- Shared perspectives
- Dominant logic
- Blindspots
- Organizational schema
- Tunnel vision
- Organizational ideologies

For example, in the arm-wrestling exercise above, all of my students were given identical instructions. But the words *arm wrestling, winner,* and *opponent* were interpreted differently by the various individuals, based on their particular mental models. For most, even the mention of words such as *winner* and *opponent* creates images of fighting and competition. From this "mental imaging" flows behavior. Most try to compete without even considering the strategy of cooperation as an option.

Mental models are important because they condition behavior. The behavior of every individual is conditioned by his or her mental model of the world.[3] Similarly, the behavior of every organization is conditioned by its dominant mental model(s).

How Mental Models Condition Behavior

Mental models can be immensely helpful because they allow us to process information and make decisions quickly. For example, if you strongly believe that it is your moral duty to fight for your country if another country attacks, you will not spend too much time mulling over the question "Should I fight for my country?" Nor will you need to undertake an elaborate cost-benefit analysis to decide whether or not to fight. You will do it simply because you strongly believe that it is the right thing to do. Your behavior is thus governed by your mental model, which says: "It is the duty of every citizen to fight for and protect his or her country."

With mental models, there is no "right" or "wrong." Nobody can claim that his or her beliefs or values are superior to yours. However, mental models can create problems, for the following two reasons:

1. Mental models allow us to think "passively"—or perhaps not at all. This is what leads us to overlook the obvious. As an example of this problem, consider the following exercise. If you count between 1 and 100, how many times will you find a number that has a 9 in it? Please take thirty seconds to think through this problem before reading any further.

When I try this exercise with my students, more than 75 percent of them come back with the answer "Ten times." When I ask for a listing of these ten numbers, a volunteer says: "9, 19, 29, 39, and so on." From the moment you say "and so on," your mind has switched from active to passive thinking. That is because you have identified the "pattern"; you know what the answer is, so why spend more time considering it? It is this kind of passive thinking that prevents most people from "seeing" the other nine possibilities: 90, 91, 92, 93, 94, 95, 96, 97, 98. The correct answer is nineteen times. It seems so obvious, yet most people overlook it.

2. The second reason why strong mental models can be problematic is the fact that human beings tend to reject new information that contradicts what they already believe. If we have very strong mental models, we tend to hear or see whatever supports our existing beliefs and ways of operating. Any new information that does

not support our beliefs is generally discarded as wrong or irrelevant. This is the number one killer of innovation in companies.

Thus, strong mental models make us think passively and keep us from adopting, or even considering, new ideas. As a final demonstration of the negative effects of strong mental models, try this exercise.

I have in mind an English word that has four letters. It's missing the first letter, but I know that it ends with the letters ___any. Can you think of a word that fits this description? When given this task, most people come up very quickly with the answer *many*—in other words, the missing letter is *m*. But now consider this problem: Same principle. I have in my mind an English word that's missing the first letter but ends with ___eny. Can you think of a word now? Please take thirty seconds to come up with one before reading further.

Most people cannot think of a word. They go through the alphabet, putting individual letters in front of the ___eny, trying to create a word they recognize. Most fail. Imagine their surprise when a volunteer shouts the answer: *deny*. Most people miss this obvious answer because they search for words that have the same vowel sound that's in *many*. The first answer in this exercise has biased our thinking and forced us to think in a very narrow way. But now think of this implication: *If one word is enough to bias our thinking in such a way, imagine what twenty or thirty years in a given business can do.*

How to Escape Mental Models

Despite having such a profound effect on our behavior, most of our individual and organizational mental models are *tacit*—they exist and govern our behavior, but we are not aware of either their existence or their influence on our actions.

The actions of an organization are also conditioned by numerous tacit mental models, or sacred cows, as they are often called. Whenever I ask executives to identify and list the sacred cows of their business, they usually provide a long laundry list, ranging from strong beliefs in what customers really want to what it takes to be successful in the business to what one can or cannot do in the business. Unnoticed and invisible, sacred cows govern the behavior of that company without its managers even realizing their existence. The more successful a company grows, the more deeply entrenched these sacred cows become, until they finally become accepted truths, never to be questioned, challenged, or debated.

The way to overcome the negative effects of these tacit mental models is to make them *visible*—that is, to bring them to the surface and question their validity and usefulness. Questioning does not necessarily mean abandoning. You might question your mental models and decide that nothing's wrong with them. The important thing is to identify and question them so as to start thinking in an active way about all those things which you take for granted.

Think about it: if the essence of strategic innovation is to discover new customers, or new products, or new ways of playing the game, how can this discovery take place if you never question who your customers really are, what your value proposition to those customers really is, or even whether your existing ways of manufacturing, distributing, and selling are still optimal? Questioning the very things we take for granted is the key to strategic innovation.

Unfortunately, as I describe in more detail in Chapter 4, simply encouraging organizations to develop a questioning attitude is not enough. For real questioning to take place, the organization often must be galvanized into active thinking through the creation of a *positive crisis*.

A positive crisis can be achieved by developing a new and ambitious objective, one that stretches the company beyond its normal capacity to act. Provided that you can convince the organization that the objective is worthwhile, people will soon realize that such an ambitious objective cannot be achieved by doing the same old things better. They will realize that to achieve such a goal they will have to think and behave differently. In fact, this is exactly what happened in the 1960s when President Kennedy challenged America to put a man on the moon before the end of the decade.

In addition, since we all know that in organizations the urgent often supercedes the important, it is not enough to convince people that questioning the status quo is merely *important*. They must be convinced that it is absolutely *urgent*. To ensure that this kind of questioning takes place on a continual basis, top management must find ways to make it a priority. Creating a positive crisis is one way. Another is to encourage top management to reward ideas that arise because somebody in the organization challenged the status quo.

In Chapter 6, I argue that to get the behaviors we want in an organization we must first create the appropriate organizational context. To motivate people to continually question the organization's sacred cows, you must first create an environment that encourages and promotes this kind of behavior. Consider, for example, this advice from Andrew Grove of Intel:

> Most helpful of all are the Cassandras in your organization: the people who tell you the bad news. Not all organizations have people telling you the bad news if you are in senior management. . . . If you want people to bring you bad news and you want to create an environment in which that is possible and encouraged, you must not create fear by punishing or penalizing in any way the bearer of bad news. If you are good that way and if your company is good that way, the people who are closest to a problem—closest to a technology, closest to a sales situation, closest to a customer situation. . . —will quickly bring them to you in management. The informational structure of the organization tends to isolate you, the manager, from field news or from first-hand news. So it is vital for you to ensure that the Cassandras bring the news to you. Sales [departments] are particularly good at being Cassandras. They are the first to get beaten up by the customers, to notice that they are losing more orders. They require access and a channel for bringing bad news to senior management so that senior management can integrate it back into the organization's overall strategy.[4]

Questioning our mental models is one way to escape their confining effect. Other tactics can also be used (see Exhibit 2-2).

Outsiders, whose mental models are different from those prevailing in an organization, can act as catalysts in prompting an organization to rethink the way it does business. Thus, the entry of a new CEO (especially if he or she comes from a totally different industry)

Exhibit 2-2   Some Tactics for Overcoming Mental Models

- Identify them and question them.

- Facilitate this questioning by developing a positive crisis in the organization.

- Utilize outsiders as catalysts for discussion.

- Replace the top management.

- Benchmark outside the industry.

- Institutionalize a questioning attitude throughout the organization.

- Experiment with new ideas.

- Provide facts or examples that go against "conventional wisdom."

- Monitor leading indicators of the company's performance.

- Seek feedback from outsiders—customers, distributors, and so on.

---

can kick-start the strategic innovation process. Active *benchmarking of outsiders* (competitors or companies in other industries) can also facilitate the active questioning of existing mental models and open the mind to other possibilities.

Another useful tactic is to develop a *questioning attitude* that continually asks, "Why?" "Why," for example, "are we selling our products in this way?" When this question is legitimized with the support of examples of organizations that are selling their products in a different way and are quite profitable, the question "Why?" can be a powerful wake-up call.

Still more tactics can be used to escape from mental models, some of them fairly obvious, though nonetheless effective: experimenting with new ideas, providing facts or examples that argue against "conventional wisdom," monitoring leading indicators of company performance, and getting feedback from parties outside the company (for example, customers and distributors). My list of tactics is not meant to be exhaustive. The important thing to note is that superior strategies very rarely emerge unless mental models are questioned and sacred cows slaughtered as necessary.

Definition of the Business:
Any Organization's Biggest Mental Model

Companies have a host of mental models, or sacred cows—the assumptions no one ever questions, the behaviors everyone takes for granted. But the most dominant mental model any company has is its *perception of what business it is in.* The definition a company gave to its business, probably a long time ago in an implicit way, today conditions the way that company sees its business, which in turn determines how that company is going to play the game in that business—that is, it determines the company's strategy.

To appreciate this point, consider the following examples. In 1989, Denis Cassidy took over as chairman and CEO of Boddington Group PLC, a vertically integrated beer producer that owned a brewery, wholesalers, and a large chain of pubs throughout Great Britain. In the next two years, Cassidy set about the task of transforming the company into a retailing and hospitality business. The first step was to give up manufacturing. Despite tremendous resistance from the family-controlled company board, Cassidy sold off the brewery. He then diversified the company, acquiring leisure hotels, restaurants, nursing homes, and health clubs while keeping the original portfolio of pubs. The basis for these strategic moves was Cassidy's belief that the company was "no longer in the brewing business" but in the retailing business:

> The decision to abandon brewing was a painful one, especially since the brewery has been a part of us for more than 200 years. But given the changes taking place in the business, we realized that we could not play the brewing game with the big boys. We decided to build on our excellent skills in retailing, hospitality, and . . . property management to start a new game.

By all accounts, Cassidy's strategy in the period 1989–94 created enormous shareholder value.

At about the same time, another British company, Blue Circle Industries PLC, one of the world's leading producers of cement, was using a very similar logic to guide its strategic moves, but with disastrous results. In the early 1980s, branching out from its core business, cement, Blue Circle diversified into a variety of other businesses: property management, brick production, waste management, industrial minerals, gas cookers, bathroom furnishings, and lawnmowers. What was the driving logic behind this all-over-the-board attempt to diversify? According to a retired senior executive:

> We started out believing that our business was not just the cement business but the supply of building materials, *one* of which is cement. This led us into the bricks business and then soon after that into cooking appliances and central heating boilers—after all, these are all products you need when you build your house with our bricks and cement. The culmination of this strategy was our move into lawnmowers, based on the logic that you need a lawnmower for your garden, which is after all next to the house which our materials built!

Needless to say, this strategy did not prove successful for Blue Circle.

Despite their divergent fortunes, Boddington and Blue Circle serve to illustrate the same simple but powerful point: Everything a company does in its business is conditioned by its perception of what its business is. This business definition is often tacit and unarticulated, but it still governs the behaviors of people in the company. Therefore, a company can only decide what to do in a business (that is, determine its strategy) after it has explicitly addressed the question, "What is our business?"

Not only is defining the business the crucial first step in strategy formulation, but *questioning the accepted definition* and possibly *re*-defining it can open up the mind to new strategic actions the company could be taking. For example, the reason Boddington's was able to "see" a different way of playing the game was because it stopped seeing itself as being in the brewing business and started seeing itself in the retailing business. Similarly, Blue Circle was able to "see" a different way of playing the game because it stopped seeing itself as being in the cement business and started seeing itself as being in the supply-of-building-materials business.

Note that I am not arguing that the act of redefining a business will in itself necessarily bring favorable results. The very fact that Blue Circle destroyed enormous value as a result of adopting the supply-of-building-materials definition should serve as a warning of the dangers of adopting broad and grand-sounding business definitions. In fact, it is exactly this practice that led thousands of U.S. corporations into a disastrous series of diversification moves between 1960 and 1980 and that is accounting for the reversal of these moves now taking place in corporate America.[5]

*Re*defining your business is no guarantee that you will find *better* ways to compete. Its purpose is to help you imagine *different* ways to compete. Whether or not "different" will be in the best interest of the company is another consideration altogether. What's most important is for the company to know that these possibilities are out there.

The importance of defining a business in an appropriate way has been recognized for a long time. Almost forty years ago, Professor Ted Levitt of Harvard Business School wrote the influential article "Marketing Myopia," quoted above. In it, he argued that U.S. railroad companies lost market share because they did not define their business properly. By taking their business to be the railroad business, they failed to see the threat posed by competitors such as airlines and buses. Levitt proposed that railroad companies would have been better off had they thought of themselves as being in the transportation business.

My argument is that Levitt was probably wrong in advising railroads to define their business in the specific manner he did—that is, as the transportation business. He was right about one thing, however: Every company needs to think through and explicitly identify (according to criteria I list in this chapter) the business it considers itself to be in.[6]

Unfortunately, most established companies have not made a conscious decision about what business they are in. This means that every move they make is influenced by a definition of which they are largely unaware. This also means that they are missing out on the most important way to strategically innovate in their business—by *re*defining it.

A fascinating illustration of the power of business redefinition was articulated by Hal Rosenbluth, president and CEO of Rosenbluth Travel.[7] In describing how he managed to transform the company from a $20 million business in 1978 to a $1.3 billion global travel management company by 1990, he says, "Our biggest advantage was to understand that as deregulation changed the rules of travel, we were no longer in the travel business so much as we were in the information business."[8] This fundamental rethinking of what business the company was in led Rosenbluth to initiate a series of actions (such as acquisitions of computers and airline reservation systems, the development of a private reservation data system, the development of customer databases) that to an outside observer must have seemed, at the very least, "strange" for an old-fashioned travel business. But to Rosenbluth these actions made perfect sense: if you are in the travel *information* business, this is what you need to do to be successful. Rosenbluth claims that the company underwent a similar transformation in 1892, when his great-grandfather had an insight into the business. He realized that "he wasn't just in travel, selling tickets to people who wanted to cross the Atlantic. He was in family immigration, getting whole clans of people successfully settled in America."[9] The importance of knowing what business you're in is not something new; it's been around as long as business itself.

Such redefinition of the business is at the heart of strategic innovation, and it is truly remarkable how many of today's strategic innovators began their revolutionary journey by first redefining the business they were in. For example, Howard Schultz, president of Starbucks, does not believe he is in the coffee business. Instead, he is in the business of creating a consumption experience, of which coffee is a part. A visit to one of his stores involves "romance, theatrics, community—the totality of the coffee experience."[10] If you are in the "experience" business rather than the coffee business, you will behave very differently from your competitors in the coffee business.

Hewitt Associates, the Chicago-based human resources consultancy, is another example of successful business redefinition. The firm has successfully moved from its traditional base of benefit and compensation consulting services to become the major provider of retirement and health plan administration and outsourcing services. According to CEO Dale Gifford, the firm's strategy is based on the notion that Hewitt is in the business of "human resources consulting and services. We unbundle and remix health plans and retirement plans for the customer. This is different from how we thought of ourselves twenty or thirty years ago. In the 1970s and 1980s, we were a benefits and compensation firm. Now, we are in the human relations business, helping our clients become more effective through their people." It's not hard to imagine how the Hewitt strategy will change by listening to Dale Gifford's definition of the future business of the firm: "In the future, we will be a general contractor for our clients—not just a subcontractor. We will offer our clients a whole system of workforce solutions."

Such redefinition of the business is possible only if the question "What business are we really in?" is asked.

The Process: How to Define and Redefine the Business (Over and Over Again)

At this point, it's important to understand that there is no one right or wrong way to define a business. Nor can you know beforehand whether a certain definition will be a winner. The whole purpose of asking the question "What business am I really in?" is to identify a specific definition that will allow you to maximize the impact of your firm's unique capabilities relative to those of your competitors. The key is to find a definition that *fits* exactly with your firm's unique capabilities. It is this fit that gives you competitive advantage, and it is this fit that determines if you have arrived at the right definition of your business. Put simply, the "right" definition of your business is one that suits your firm better than it does your competitors. Thus, what is a good definition for your company may be completely inappropriate for another company, and what is a good definition for your competitor—given its particular strengths—may be equally inappropriate for you. What makes a definition "good" is in the eyes of the beholder.

The important thing is to ask the question, consider the implications of a possible redefinition, assess what new tactics should be adopted if you were to redefine, consider whether your core competencies will allow you to carry out these tactics efficiently, and so on. Thus, the purpose of asking the question is to trigger proactive thinking.

There are three schools of thought on how to define a business. Traditionally, companies have defined their business *according to the product* they were selling. Thus, Ford was in the car business, Boeing was in the airplane business, and Philip Morris was in the cigarette business.

This way of defining a business came under severe attack in the early 1960s, following the critical assault by Theodore Levitt in "Marketing Myopia." Levitt argued that a business that is defined by its product is too narrowly defined. He championed the notion that a company should define its business *according to the customer function* it is trying to fulfill. Levitt emphasized the importance of customers and encouraged companies to identify the *underlying functionality* of their products. By asking, "What benefits does the customer derive from my product?" a company can identify its true value-added and thus define its business. In other words, if your company was Ford, instead of thinking you were in the car business, you should think of it as the transport business or the family entertainment business or whatever other function your product is fulfilling.

Recently, a third perspective has emerged, in which companies are encouraged to define their business *according to their portfolio of core competencies.*[11] For example, Sony might want to argue that it is in the business of selling "pocketable" products, and Apple that it is in the business of selling "user friendliness."

None of these three basic approaches to defining a business is the "right" one. Each has its merits and limitations. A terrific definition for one company may be a terrible one for another—it all depends on each company's unique capabilities and on which definition allows the company to employ its capabilities in the best possible way and thus gain competitive advantage relative to its competitors. As a quick demonstration of this simple truth, compare what Ted Levitt advised in "Marketing Myopia" with what Hermann Simon reported about successful German companies in his 1996 book *Hidden Champions*. Levitt said that U.S. railroad companies defined their business too narrowly. They thought they were in the railroad business when they should have realized they were really in the transport business. As a result, he contended, the railroads lost market share to companies that were in the transport business: the airlines, bus lines, trucking, and so on. Yet Simon argued that the reason small German companies have been so successful in the last forty years is precisely *because* they defined their businesses in a narrow way and then proceeded to dominate their respective niches around the globe.[12]

The secret of strategic innovation is not the adoption of any one of these three approaches—rather, it involves examining each one to see which makes for the best fit for your firm. The breakthrough usually comes when a company confronts its "dominant" way of defining its business (which is, say, customer driven) with a new approach (say, product driven). This forces the firm to confront a "new" situation, where the answers are not known already and nothing is taken for granted. This sudden confrontation with a new reality forces the mind to abandon its passive ways and start thinking actively.

A Way of Doing It

The thinking process a company should go through to define and redefine its business consists of four steps:

1. List all possible definitions of the business. (For example, the list for BMW might look like this: we are in the car business, the prestige car business, the transport business, the ego business, the business of satisfying the transport needs of yuppies, the driving business, the engineering business, the up-market global car business, and so on.) Make the list as long as you can and try to include definitions that are product-, customer- and competence-based. To develop this list, ask for the opinions of "outsiders"—such as your customers, your distributors, or even the person in the street who may have heard of your company.

2. Evaluate each definition according to a series of criteria.[13] These are the most pertinent: If I define my business as X, who are my customers and what do they need? Who are my competitors? Can I satisfy these customer needs in a unique (better) way relative to my competitors? Given this definition, am I capable of maintaining a competitive advantage? Is my definition of the market "attractive" (that is, likely to grow in the future, protected by barriers, and so on)? What will be the key success factors in this "business"? Can I deliver? How do my competitors behave, and what does that imply about how they have defined the business? Does this definition allow me to satisfy my personal objectives for the company? Is

what I have defined as my business what my customers think is my business? *The same series of questions should be used to evaluate each definition.* The goal is to identify the definition that gives your company maximum leverage relative to competitors.

3. Choose one definition. This is a crucial step. Making a choice implies facing certain follow-up decisions. It implies, for example, that the company will invest in certain products or in subsidiaries in certain countries and not in others. It also implies that certain managers will "lose out" in the next budget round and some will "win." Because of the uncomfortable consequences of such choices, most companies fudge the issue. Yet a clear and explicit decision is exactly what the organization needs.

Consider, for example, the decision by Texas Instruments in the early 1970s to redefine its business from the "semiconductor business" to the "consumer electronics business." According to an article published in *Newsweek* in 1978, the company decided to "put most of its development money for the next few years into the consumer business rather than into computer memories and microprocessors, as its competitors did." J. Fred Bucy, the president and CEO at the time was quoted as saying, "We penalized semiconductors—that was the price for allocating our resources."[14]

4. Finish your thinking by asking this question: If a competitor were to redefine the business, what would its resulting strategy be? Into what actions would that strategy be translated? How can I prepare for such an event?

This last step is as important as the previous three. There's always the possibility that your competitor will redefine the business before you do. You must be on the lookout for competitors that have redefined the business in a way that's appropriate for them. By asking "What if my competitor redefined the business?" you'll be able to recognize the event should it take place (as evidenced in the actions of the competitor) and then act quickly. Early detection allows for a more effective response to maverick competitors.

Even if none of your competitors redefines the business, it is still important to understand their current, working definitions of their business. This analysis tells you what they consider to be their heartland: the customers they target, the products they emphasize, the investments they believe they must make. By implication, it also tells you about which customers they will *not* pursue, which products they will *not* make, and which investments they will *not* undertake. In other words, this analysis can be used to predict your competitors' future behavior. You might use it to predict a competitor's likely response to a specific move you are about to make. Similarly, you can use it to identify the kinds of products or customers your competitor might be willing to give up without too much of a fight. You can then target these customers or products yourself.

These four steps represent the kind of process a company should go through in deciding how to define its business. Imagine the power of revisiting these questions every year or two. In particular, imagine the power of asking the follow-up question: "Have any changes occurred that make another definition of the business more attractive to the company?" This is the source of strategic innovation—just when everybody else has settled into a certain accepted definition and behaves accordingly, you "discover" a new definition that allows you to start playing the game differently and catch everyone else off-guard. Of course, to "discover" a new definition you must continually be searching for one.

The problem is that very few companies actually decide in an explicit way what business they are in, let alone start thinking about how to redefine the business. Yet making this determination is the most important element of any strategy. Even the few companies that do so often fail to make a specific decision when the time comes or, having made the decision ("This is the business I will be in"), fail to revisit it, believing that it is cast in concrete, never to be questioned again.

The Case of Pegasus Tour Operator

The experience of a leading travel and tour operator in the early 1990s provides an example of how attempts to redefine a business can play out in real life. In the interest of confidentiality, I'll call this British company Pegasus Tour Operator. Pegasus offered, among other products and services, tours to the Aegean Islands using its own boats. Its primary customers were tourists who wanted to visit the islands while on vacation.

Pegasus had been the market leader in this competitive field for most of its thirty-five years of existence. In the early 1990s, however, it began losing market share at an alarming rate to two competitors. The first was an established Italian player offering extremely low prices—so low, in fact, that Pegasus managers had a hard time seeing how the company was making any profit. The second was a start-up from Greece that competed on the basis of a "bigger," "superior" product. It promised to take customers not only to the Aegean Islands but to the whole of the Eastern Mediterranean, including Egypt, Israel, and Cyprus.

Pegasus hired a prestigious consulting company for advice on how to respond to these competitors. The consultants recommended that Pegasus buy bigger boats, so that it could offer customers the bigger package the second competitor was offering. At the same time, the consultants advised Pegasus on how to reduce its operating costs; any reductions in costs would be passed on to customers in the form of lower prices, which was to give Pegasus an edge over its Italian counterpart.

Pegasus pursued this strategy for four years without a significant increase in its market share. In early 1995, Pegasus decided to abandon this strategy in favor of another: to focus on customers who were primarily interested in the Greek islands and to make their experience on these islands as exciting as possible. This decision led the company managers to sell their bigger boats and replace them with smaller, more modern models; to introduce onboard entertainment, including trained historians who would explain the history of each island to be visited; and to arrange for special meals featuring each island's cuisine. Judging from the financial results of the last two years, this strategy has been successful.

What kind of thinking on the part of Pegasus may have motivated the above actions? First, observe that the other two companies were competing on the basis of a business definition different from that adopted by Pegasus. Pegasus was operating under this definition: "I am in the business of providing tours to the Greek islands." This conception of its business led it to adopt a particular strategy that for nearly thirty-five years proved to be very successful.

Along came the Italian competitor, serving the same islands but offering cheap prices. On further examination, Pegasus learned that this competitor was able to offer such low prices because its boats carried not only tourists but also materials such as food and construction supplies for the islands. This competitor had been in the transport business in Italy before entering the Aegean Islands tourist market. The owner of the company was able to imagine the potential of utilizing the boats for transport of both materials and tourists because *transport*, as he saw it, was his business. With this definition in mind and the boats (and the strategy) ready to go, he was poised to play the transport game well. Needless to say, this strategy also meant that this competitor could neither move its boats as fast as Pegasus nor offer as many trips per day. However, in all of its advertising campaigns, the Italian competitor emphasized its low prices and was careful to avoid mention of these relative weaknesses.

The success of the other new competitor (the Greek start-up) stemmed from a different definition of the business. As far as its managers were concerned, this company was in the business of "offering tours to all of the Eastern Mediterranean." In other words, it was offering a different experience in more exotic destinations than Pegasus. This definition led the firm to purchase different kinds of boats and to adopt a strategy intended to serve vacationers interested in such tours.

Thus, even though all three competitors appeared to be in the same business, they were really operating under the influence of different definitions. Notice that I am not saying that one definition is better than the others; all three are feasible. The question is, what should Pegasus do given its adopted definition and the fact that it was losing market share?

Pegasus could of course have decided to change its business definition and adopt one of the others on offer. (In fact, the consultants' advice amounted to that.) However, the fact that other companies are playing the game in a certain way and winning does *not* mean that every company should play the game that way. The questions that Pegasus managers should have asked themselves right from the start are these: "Which game are we really good at? Where do we have unique strengths that allow us to gain a competitive advantage over our competitors?" After asking these questions, they realized that Pegasus had operated in the Aegean for so many years that it had accumulated a lot of knowledge about the islands, their customs, and their history and about the best way to ferry people from one to the other (such as which routes were best depending on the time of year).

This line of thought led Pegasus to the conclusion that it was time to give up the old competitive game for a new one: that of providing customers with "a unique vacation *experience.*" Taking people from one island to another quickly and efficiently was just one element of the strategy. Pegasus could do many other things to enhance its customers' vacation experience, such as providing history lessons and samples of the local cuisine. The company also had to communicate its new definition to customers, telling them, in effect, "Yes, you can go with Company X, which is cheaper, or Company Y, which is bigger, or you can go with us and become immersed in the culture and history of the islands, benefiting from our thirty-five year history as island tour guides."

Many other actions flowed from this starting point. For example, the decision to focus on the "experience" rather than the "trip" led Pegasus to target a new customer base, to adopt a totally different marketing campaign, and to hire completely different people. The specific actions the company took followed from the initial redefinition of the business. Once this definition was adopted, what had to be done became obvious.

A caveat: What Pegasus did was ask itself "What game are we really good at?" and then focus on that game. But there is a danger associated with this kind of thinking: it is inward looking. What happens if the game has changed so that what the company has to offer is no longer what is needed to be successful? What happens if its core competencies are inadequate or irrelevant to the competitive realities of the market today? Or tomorrow?

What can be done to avoid the danger of being too self-absorbed? Management can try to predict how the industry is going to change and build the necessary competencies accordingly. Or management can build a variety of competencies into the firm now, hoping that however the future unfolds, the company will be prepared to compete. Both approaches require the organization to recognize the importance of learning and to put in place structures and processes that facilitate such learning throughout the organization (the importance and facilitation of learning is covered in detail in Chapters 8 and 9). Competition is a never-ending game, and any advantage a company has will eventually be eroded unless it takes every opportunity to learn and apply new strategies.

This is not to say that a company shouldn't do its best to leverage its current competencies. Obviously, it was exactly this kind of thinking that allowed Pegasus to succeed. So a company needs to make the most of what it has in the present to play the game now, while at the same time considering and developing new strategies for the games that will unfold in the future. It's not a matter of doing one or the other. Both must be done. This is a major strategic issue for any company, and we will return to it in Chapter 9.

The Pegasus strategy was a dramatic success. It rejuvenated the company and restored its leadership position. But this doesn't mean that the way Pegasus defined itself was necessarily "better" than the ways the other two companies defined themselves (if, in fact, they did). Nor does it mean that this definition alone is enough to guarantee Pegasus's continued success. Rather, Pegasus is a good example of the key points made in this chapter.

Summary

1. What we need to do in a business (that is, our strategy) is conditioned by what we think that business is. An essential element of any strategy should be the clear and explicit definition of the business the company is in. Formulating this definition should be the starting point of any strategy-planning session. Once you have a specific definition, the actions you need to take become apparent.

2. There is no right or wrong way to define a business. The trick is to identify a definition that suits your company's unique capabilities. Doing so allows the company to maximize the impact of its unique capabilities relative to competitors and gives it the competitive advantage it needs to be profitable.

3. Once accepted, a business definition must be questioned continually. As business conditions change, another definition may become more attractive. Unless a company is willing to question its current

definition and explore alternatives, these potentially more attractive definitions will never be discovered.

4. Often the most dangerous competitors are mavericks—companies that break the rules of the game. What allows them to "see" a way of competing that's different from that of established competitors is a different starting point—a different definition of the business. The only way to compete with mavericks is to identify their "new" behavior early on in the game. To do that, a firm must be on constant alert. It is only by correctly identifying their business definitions that you will be able to make sense of their behavior as well as recognize their maverick behavior early on in the game.

5. A business definition that works well for one firm will not necessarily work for another; there should be no rush to imitate. Each firm should adopt the definition that makes sense for itself, given its unique capabilities.

Decide Who Your Customers Are and What to Offer Them

The customer is frequently wrong. We don't carry those sorts of customers. We write them and say: "Fly somebody else."

—Herb Kelleher, CEO, Southwest Airlines

Being great at everything is not an actionable message."

—Floris Maljers, former Unilever chief executive

In 1979, Emerson Electric acquired the Skil corporation, a leading manufacturer of power tools. Soon after, Skil embarked on a radical new strategy, the main components of which were the decisions to (1) drastically narrow the product range and (2) transfer its selling efforts from big department stores (like Sears) to hardware stores. In the short term, this decision led to millions of dollars in lost sales. "Losing" a big customer such as Sears or Kmart is tough, and convincing the sales force of the wisdom of selling a much narrower product portfolio (especially when Skil's competitor, Black & Decker, was expanding its portfolio) was not easy.

After an initial dip, however, sales quickly picked up, and within five years it became apparent that the new strategy was a winner. In fact, it was so successful that excluded stores such as Sears and Kmart started pleading with Skil to buy its products. In the words of William L. Davis, then president of Skil: "We had Wal-Mart, Kmart, Home Depot, Builders' Square beating our doors down to try and buy Skil products, and we turned them down. We turned down $100 million [annually] in business easily if we had taken them on."[1]

What led to this happy state of affairs? First, the choice of hardware stores as exclusive distributors helped create an up-market image for the product: hardware stores are where "professionals" are thought to buy their tools, so the Skil product developed a professional image. Second, the hardware stores were thrilled that the end-consumer could not simply walk down the street to their retail competitors to buy the Skil products. As a result, they actively promoted the Skil products in their stores. The combination of these factors rejuvenated Skil, propelling the company to a strong position in the business.[2]

This example highlights a simple point: the choice of customer and the choice of products or services are strategic choices. It is the company's strategic responsibility to decide who will be its customer and what products it will offer that customer. *Unless the company has unlimited resources, it cannot be everything to everybody.* The world's best universities understand this: every year they decline to accept as "customers" more than 80 percent of those who want to "buy" their product. In this sense, they are exercising one of the greatest powers any organization has—that of selecting its customers strategically.

An essential element of any strategy is the explicit consideration of these two questions: *Who* should we target as customers? *What* should we offer them? Unfortunately, very few companies pose these questions during a strategy session. For example, when was the last time your company got rid of a customer—especially a profitable one—because you decided that customer was not the "right" one for your company? When was the last time you identified a new customer segment that everyone else had overlooked? When was the last time your company was the first to introduce *the* product that everyone wanted to buy?

These things do not happen by accident. The companies that do discover new, unexploited customer segments (The Body Shop, Southwest Airlines) or do come up with new winning products that nobody else—including the customer—had thought about (Sony's walkman, Yamaha's electronic pianos) are not just "lucky." These wonderful things happen only to companies that consider the "who" and "what" questions in a strategic manner.

A company needs to consider these questions strategically because the answers to them will establish the parameters within which the company will operate. By definition, these answers also determine the terrain in which the company does *not* operate. Ultimately, they determine where the company will invest its money and where it won't.

But these answers are not cast in concrete. Innovation in strategy will most likely take place when a company questions its answers to these questions. Just as a company should never be complacent in its judgment of what business it is in (per Chapter 2), it must never be complacent in its judgment of who it considers to be its customers and what it understands to be its products or services. Questioning the answers to "who" and "what" is a way for a company to open its eyes to new customer segments and new product ideas. Pursuing a superior strategy involves continually questioning the answers to these questions and continually experimenting with new ideas that result from this process.

Who Is Our Customer?

Ideally, a company wants to sell its products to everyone—the more the merrier! Unfortunately, it cannot afford to market to everyone. If that were not so, then every company would be a global company trying to sell its wares to everyone all around the world.

Assuming that a company does not have unlimited resources (money, managerial time, and the like), it has to decide where to focus the limited ones it does have. Granted, there are always potentially lucrative customers and new opportunities to pursue. Having to home in on only a few is perhaps unfortunate, but necessary. If a company shies away from making a clear choice—because the pool of customers simply looks too good to pass up or because the company wants to remain "flexible," keeping all its options "open"—it will pursue an unfocused strategy that wastes valuable resources. In trying to be master of all, a company is likely to become master of none.

I use the term *customer* in all its variants. For some companies, people like you and me are the customer—for example, the home furnishings company IKEA sells directly to you and me. Other companies have corporations as customers—for example, Intel sells its processors to Compaq, Dell, IBM, and other PC makers.

Yet other companies have industries (or even nations) as customers—for example, Honeywell sells to the car, oil, and aerospace industries (among others). But no matter who your customer is, the idea that you need to select your customer strategically still applies.

To make the decision about what customers to focus on, a company will have to consider two questions (see Exhibit 3-1):

1. Who are the *possible* customers it *could be* selling to? Determining this universe requires creativity. Most breakthroughs in strategy originate from this point, yet it is easy to stymie the potential gains by sticking to preconceived notions (mental models) and stereotypes. Unless you are willing to question the existing "packaged" answers as to who your customer really is, chances are that you will identify the same old customer segments that you (and all of your competitors) have been serving all along.

2. Of all these potential customers, which *should* it target? To determine this, you need to develop a set of criteria to evaluate all the possible customers and then decide which ones are the "right" ones for your company.

Exhibit 3-1   Deciding on the "Who"

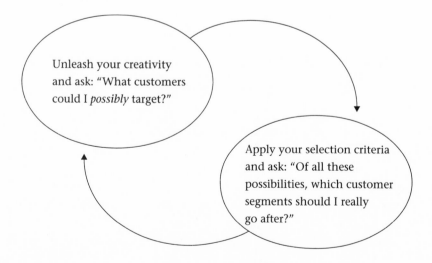

The thinking process used to settle these issues is *not* (and should not be) linear. You could start your thinking by answering the first question and then moving to the second. But you could also start by developing the criteria by which you will evaluate potential customers and then use those criteria to identify the most attractive customers. You could do this by asking the question, "Given these criteria, who out there can be an attractive customer for my company?" Once initiated, the process should be creative and generative, with each of the two steps in the process contributing to the other.

Identifying Possible Customers: Think Creatively

Identifying possible customers essentially means that the firm has to consider what *geographic region* and *customer segments* to serve. First, think about geographic region. What part of the globe will you focus on? Will you sell in the United States only? Or perhaps in the United States and a few selected European countries? Or maybe in the United States and Europe and Japan? You have to make a choice. Next, think about segments. Which specific customer groups will you focus on? Will you sell only to the rich? Or to the rich and the middle class? Will you target big companies or small ones? High-tech or low-tech? Mature or growing? Here again, you have to choose.[3]

For example, brokerage firm Edward Jones made a very explicit choice as to what customers to target. The firm goes after individual rather than institutional investors and targets individuals who live in defined "communities." In the early days, the firm targeted individuals who lived in small towns in the Midwest. And even now that the firm is expanding into big cities, it still focuses on areas in those cities that are characterized by a "sense of community." Managing principal John Bachmann puts it bluntly: "I am not interested in New York City. I am interested in Greenwich. I'm not interested in London—how can I put my hands around it? I am interested in Chelsea or Fulham. . . ."

Similarly, the small Danish bank Lan & Spar has made clear and explicit choices about what customers to focus on, by both segment and geographic region. In 1989, the bank specifically asked all of its corporate clients (who accounted for 25 percent of its deposits) to leave the bank and open accounts with its competitors. As CEO Peter Schou puts it: "I simply wrote a letter to all of our corporate clients and asked them to move their accounts to another bank." Lan & Spar had decided to target white-collar workers instead, even though they represented only 20 percent of the Danish working population. Naturally, this decision led to a sharp decline in the bank's market share, but within a year new customers were opening accounts at Lan & Spar in droves. By 1991, Lan & Spar emerged as the most profitable bank in Denmark. Today, it is still one of the most profitable banks in the country, and its market share has quadrupled since the change in customer focus was initiated in 1989. In a similar vein, the bank has repeatedly rejected suggestions to export its successful formula to other Scandinavian countries. According to Shou, the bank will, "for the time being at least, concentrate on the Danish market and reject temptations to move into other countries." Schou believes there are still enough opportunities to be exploited in Denmark and that Lan & Spar has no need to go looking for them in other countries.

Consider also Chicago-based consulting group Hewitt Associates. According to CEO Dale Gifford:

> Four years ago, we discovered that out of the 3,000 clients we had, 400 accounted for about 60 percent of our total business and an even greater percentage of our profits. So, we decided to focus even more attention on these successful customers. Our substantial additional investments are geared toward these clients so that we understand what they really need and we spend more time with them developing even stronger business partnerships. As for the other group of customers—we still serve most of them, but we do not invest much extra time or resources on them. We do not try to aggressively sell new additional services there. As a result, this group of less important customers has not grown at all, whereas the target group is now 80 percent of our revenues and growing rapidly. This is a tough discipline, especially in the outsourcing business. We get too many opportunities there and we cannot pursue all of them. We need to be selective.

Identifying possible customers requires creativity. Any customer base can be divided into an almost infinite number of segments, depending on how open and creative a company is in approaching the task. The reason for thinking about segmentation is to "re-segment" the established customer base in a creative way, so as to discover new segments that no one else has thought of. The company can then target its offerings in such a way that it does a better job of serving these customer segments than do its competitors.

An example of such creative resegmentation of the market is provided by a once little-known company named Enterprise Rent-A-Car. Today, Enterprise is the biggest car rental firm in the United States. It achieved this position by riding on the back of a strategy that focused not on the traditional customer segment (people who rent cars at airports) but on the customer segment of people who rent cars not only at airports but anywhere (whenever they need a car). Accordingly, Enterprise has positioned its 2,400 offices within 15 minutes of 70 percent of America's population, and it picks up customers at their homes at no extra cost.[4]

Another example of creative segmentation is provided by Dell. In selling to the home-PC market, the company did *not* want to attract first-time computer buyers as its customers because these people typically need a lot of support and service, both of which are costly. Instead, the company targeted experienced individuals who require limited support and who tend to utilize the help provided by their own company's computer department. How did Dell manage to attract one type of customer and not the other? Simple: by pricing its low-end machines more expensively than its principal competitors, such as Gateway, and pricing its high-end models less expensively than Gateway. Thus, first-time buyers who go for low-end models prefer the cheaper Gateway models, while experienced users who buy more advanced machines go for the Dell models, which are cheaper than Gateway's.

Creative segmentation of the existing customer base is one of those activities that everybody pays lip service to but very few companies have the courage to experiment with. Yet numerous examples suggest that the fastest growing companies in any business tend to be those which "happen upon" an untapped customer segment. It is easy in hindsight to recognize a fast-growing customer segment. Unfortunately, by that time all of your competitors will have recognized it too, and moved in for the kill. If you want to be the first to spot a new segment, you have to be willing to abandon preconceived notions of who your customer is and experiment with new segments.

How, then, can a company be creative in its approach to the task of identifying possible customers? One way is to fundamentally question its existing mental models as to who the customer is. To do this, you need to think beyond the products or services you sell; you need to identify the underlying functionality of the product. You should ask the question, "What customer *needs* is our product satisfying?" and then try to think of customers you're not serving now who have similar needs.[5]

Another way to think more creatively at this stage is to begin thinking from different "starting points." More often than not, a company's notion of what possible customers exist out there is severely constrained by its current line of products. In other words, most people think like this: "We make product ABC. Who out there might be a customer for this product of ours?" You can start your thinking this way, but there are other ways, too. For example, after developing the criteria for choosing the right customers, you could use them to identify all the people or companies that you want to have as customers. You then ask the question: "According to our criteria, customer XYZ is exactly the type of customer we want. What shall we do to attract this customer?" (This idea is touched on in Exhibit 3-1.)

Similarly, the decision about "who" your customer is cannot be made independent from the decision about "what" you are selling. As mentioned above, the thinking process involved in answering the "who" and the "what" questions is not and should not be linear. Sometimes you need to think like this: "I have decided to target XYZ as a customer. Now I need to know what XYZ wants so I can offer it to them." At other times, you may instead need to think like this: "I have decided to offer the products (or services) ABC. Who out there will be a good customer for these products?" Strategic innovation happens when you can switch your thinking from one line of thought to the other. It is this capacity to change tracks that allows you to escape preconceived notions of your customer and your product or service, freeing you to think actively and creatively.

Identifying Selection Criteria: Suit Yourself First

Such creative resegmentation of the market is the stuff of strategic innovation, and we will return to it later in the book, in Chapter 8. But first we must consider what criteria to use to decide if a customer is right or wrong for the company.

One of Honeywell's products is controls for the central heating and central air conditioning units of hotels. Ideally, the company would like every hotel in the world to buy its controls from Honeywell. These wishes notwithstanding, Honeywell cannot afford to market to each and every hotel around the world. It has a limited number of salespeople, who have a limited budget of money and time. Honeywell needs to decide which hotels its sales staff should visit and which they should not visit. How can the company determine which hotels are worth the time and effort?

Most companies do not have an explicit set of criteria for choosing their customers. But even the few that do tend to use criteria that describe the intrinsic characteristics of the customer. For example, they prefer customers who are profitable, who pay on time, who are growing, who are ethical, who are willing to pay a premium price, who are loyal, who are large, who have a good reputation, and so on. The question is: "Doesn't everybody want to have such customers?" Suppose you and your competitors all go after these desirable customers; for how long do you think they will remain desirable? They will certainly start playing you against your competitors and drive your prices down.

Clearly, then, deciding on whether a customer is right for your company involves looking beyond the intrinsic characteristics of the customer. You must also look at your own unique collection of assets and capabilities and decide, given these particular competencies, whether you can do more for a selected customer than your competitors can do. At the end of the day, *a "good" customer is one that values what your company can uniquely provide.* If the customer values what you have to offer, and if no other competitor can offer that customer such a good deal, that customer will be loyal, willing to pay a premium, willing to pay on time, and so on.

Because different companies have different core competencies, what may be a good customer for one company is not necessarily a good customer for another. In this sense, defining a "good" customer is very similar to defining what business you're in, as discussed in Chapter 2—that is, there is no right or wrong way to define a good customer. The whole purpose of asking the question is to identify a specific definition (be it narrow or broad) that will allow you to *maximize the impact of your unique capabilities relative to those of your competitors*. The key is to find a customer whose needs fit your unique capabilities. It is this fit that gives you competitive advantage, and it is this fit that determines whether the chosen customer will be a profitable one. Put simply, the right way to define a good customer is to pick a definition that suits you better than it does your competitors. This is why it is so important to be creative in segmenting the customer base.

Given all that's been discussed above, then, what hotels should Honeywell target? If we were to ask Honeywell what it considers to be its unique capability, it would most likely point to its technological know-how, which translates into high-quality controls. Honeywell might well boast that "If our controls are good enough for the space shuttle [which they are], they must be good enough for your hotel, too!" Now the question becomes, "Which type of hotel will really value having high-quality central heating controls that will allow it to maintain a pleasant and consistent temperature in its rooms?" The most likely answer will be hotels that consider offering this kind of comfort to *their* customers to be a key element of their service—in other words, five-star hotels. Honeywell should therefore start selling to these types of hotels. If it has more resources available, it could then target four-star and three-star hotels.

Making Use of Selection Criteria: Avoid Some Common Missteps

After listing your customer selection criteria, you must decide how to use them (see Exhibit 3-2). The first priority is to evaluate the existing customer base and distinguish those customers which are right for you and those which are not. Then take action, possibly discontinuing to sell, or at least to market, to the least valuable customers. If they decide to leave as a result, so much the better. In addition, you may want to pursue more aggressively those customers classified as "right." The second priority is to use the criteria

Exhibit 3-2 How to Use the Customer Selection Criteria

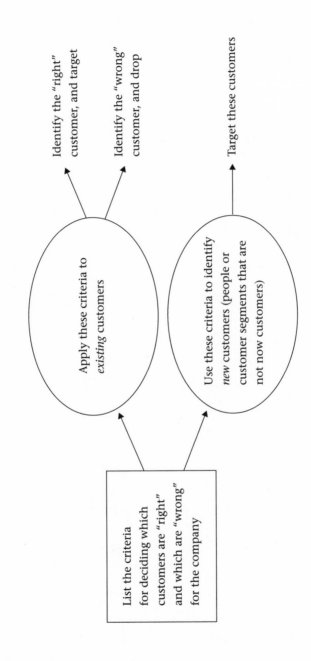

List the criteria for deciding which customers are "right" and which are "wrong" for the company

Apply these criteria to *existing* customers

Identify the "right" customer, and target

Identify the "wrong" customer, and drop

Use these criteria to identify *new* customers (people or customer segments that are not now customers)

Target these customers

to identify potential customers that match your company's definition of "right." These customers can then become the focus of the
company's marketing and selling efforts.

What if a customer that you did not target approaches your
company? Should you sell to this customer? The answer is, "It depends." If the customer satisfies the selection criteria, there is no
reason why you should not take on that customer. The important
thing is that you do not "waste" the company's limited resources
on a customer that you did not put through the process of strategic
selection.

In using these criteria, companies go through a set of predictable
"traps." Trap 1 is forgetting that every customer exacts an opportunity cost. Whenever a company is advised to get rid of a particular
customer, the usual response is, "But we are making money on this
customer! OK, it's not a lot of money, but we're still making a
profit. Why get rid of the customer?" The problem with this response is that people forget that satisfying a customer costs time
and money. Could the company get a greater rate of return by investing this time and money in another customer instead?

This line of thought was put to excellent use by Lan & Spar. The
most crucial element of the new strategy CEO Peter Schou put in
place in 1989 was that of "encouraging" more than 50 percent of
the bank's existing customers to switch to competing banks. Even
though most of these customers were profitable, the bank decided
that they were only *marginally* profitable and that its efforts would
be better spent on a particular segment of the Danish population:
young, computer-literate professionals. From this decision flowed a
series of specific actions, all intended to provide those select customers with better service than they could get from any other bank
in Denmark. Success followed from there.

Trap 2 is shying away from making the tough decisions. This is
especially true of the decision to discontinue existing customers or
to say "No" to certain prospective customers. Even if the company
has determined a particular customer is wrong for the company,
there always seems to be the hope that in the future this customer
will turn around and become right. The argument, then, is to stick
with this customer just a little longer until its attractiveness becomes plain for all to see! An even worse variant of this trap occurs

when a company acknowledges that a customer is a bad investment but decides to keep the customer for "strategic reasons." These so-called strategic reasons, however, are never articulated. Needless to say, both rationalizations can be used to justify just about anything.

Trap 3 is becoming mired in internal politicking. The decision to pursue a customer brings with it important investment and budgetary implications. For example, if a company decides to target young people in France as opposed to young people in Germany, it will be allocating investment money to France at the expense of Germany. Needless to say, this decision will not come as welcome news for the German subsidiary or its managers. Similarly, if the company decides to target young rich people (in its home country) as opposed to old rich people, the kinds of products or services it will invest in will necessarily be different. As a result, some managers in the organization will "lose out" and some will "gain" in the rounds of budget making.

Such situations are fertile ground for politicking and for debates that are doomed to be forever undecided. They usually lead to compromises that have no basis in the underlying economics or the criteria that the company developed to select good customers. The compromises are made, instead, on the basis of power and politics in the organization. An even worse outcome is indecision, reflected in statements such as this: "We need more information to make a decision on this one." It takes strong leadership to rise above the politics and force a decision.

A fascinating example of how these things play out in practice is provided by the ABC corporation (name disguised), a multibillion dollar multinational company in the business of delivering "time-sensitive" documents and parcels. During the 1995 budget discussion, which was attended by managers from every country in which the firm did business, the manager from Japan asked for an investment allocation of $100 million. His argument was that the company had only a tiny share of a Japanese market that was growing at a rate of more than 45 percent a year. This meant that with the right investment, the company had much to gain in Japan.

Judging from the general nodding of heads around the room, it appeared that the other managers were impressed by the logic of the argument. That is, until the vice president in Europe jumped in with a counterproposal: invest the money in Europe instead, he argued. Even though the European market was growing at a rate of only 6 percent per year, the company had a dominant position in Europe which should be protected. "Europe is our heartland," he reasoned. "This is where we should be investing our money if we want it to remain a dominant player."

Here's a classic situation in which a difficult choice must be made. Both arguments sound rational and logical. Both deserve careful evaluation. But, painful as it may be, a choice has to be made, one way or the other. Yes, ideally the company would prefer to invest in both markets. Yes, ideally it should want to keep its European customers without losing such an attractive opportunity in Japan. Unfortunately, the company did not have the financial means to support both options. Hence the need for a choice. As it happened (and managers everywhere will recognize this outcome right away), the CEO asked for more analysis. One month later, it was decided to allocate the money 50/50. A perfect compromise intended to keep everybody happy but that ended up short-shrifting both markets, so that neither was exploited to its potential.

This desire to keep all options open (which in reality means failure to make a choice) is a recipe for disaster. For example, in the early 1980s, Intel had to choose between its traditional CISC chip technology and the new kid on the block, RISC technology. According to Andrew Grove, Intel's CEO and president:

> Everybody in the industry thought [the RISC architecture] was going to revolutionize the design of microprocessors. Half of our people thought so, too—but the other half did not think so. So we hedged. "Can we afford not to pursue both options?" Once somebody asks that question, run for cover, because the answer is always "Of course not." Therefore, you pursue both options, which means you pursue the right option with half of your resources, because the other half of the resources are working on the wrong option. So you almost guarantee that neither option will work. That is what we did for a long period: pursuing RISC technology and non-RISC technology. Finally, at the eleventh hour, we woke up and killed the RISC project and moved everybody onto the standard Intel Architecture Project. We managed to pull out of it, but another half a year of dithering and hedging could have lost us a whole market position."[6]

Trap 4 is failing to provide a clear answer to the question of who is a good customer, not for political reasons but because the decision is not clear-cut. Trade-offs must often be made. For example, customer X may satisfy one criterion (being profitable) but fail another (being ethical). In situations such as these (which arise more often than not), the company will decide according to the weights it assigns to the various criteria. Weighting the criteria is not easy, however, and individual managers may assign different weights to each criterion. Although this is a reflection of honest differences of opinion rather than political maneuvering, the result will be debate, indecision, and calls for more information. Again, strong leadership is required to salvage the situation.

Assigning Responsibility for Decision Making: Take It from the Top

The decision as to which customers the company should target must be made at the highest level of the organization. Yes, input from everyone in the organization (or at least a diverse set of people) must be sought. Yes, the flow of information and ideas from the bottom to the top of the organization must be facilitated so that "a new idea [does not] take two years to fight its way up through endless ranks of stodgy, uncomprehending managers."[7] And yes, people must be given some flexibility to experiment beyond the customers you have decided to target. But it is ultimately the CEO who must decide who will be the company's target customers and who will not be its customers. It may turn out that the CEO made the wrong decision, but that is no excuse for failing to make a decision.

This appears to be a simple point, but it needs to be emphasized. It is common nowadays to hear the argument that the people at the front of the organization are closer to customers and have a better sense of how they are changing and what opportunities may be emerging in the market. Therefore, the logic runs, in today's fast-changing environments, where speed and agility are paramount, those frontline people should be given a prominent role in deciding which customers to pursue and what products to sell.

This is dangerous advice. An even more dangerous variant is to suggest that frontline staff should take it on themselves to target new customers or to redirect investments into new product or market areas, allowing new winning strategies simply to "emerge." Consider, for example, the following description, from a leading scholar of strategy, of how such strategies emerge:

> Out in the field, a salesman visits a customer. The product isn't quite right, and together they work out some modifications. The salesman returns to his company and puts the changes through; after two or three more rounds, they finally get it right. A new product emerges, which eventually opens up a new market. The company has changed strategic course.[8]

This is the stuff that strategic disasters are made of. Initiatives such as these can mean one of two things. Either top management has failed to articulate clearly the parameters within which the troops in the field can operate, or it has failed to determine what the parameters are in the first place, let alone communicate them to the troops. As a result, people in the field take it upon themselves to make these decisions, a clear demonstration of the lack of leadership that can lead to confusion or worse. Consider, for example, Intel's CISC versus RISC debates, as described by Andrew Grove:

> During the 1980s, a middle-level technical manager had developed the i860 RISC chip within Intel and had convinced several higher-level managers of its commercial potential. . . . The managers involved in the i860 project launched a successful marketing effort and top management had little real choice but to adopt the i860 as a new strategic product. Commercial success subsequently slowed down in the face of the competition of a plethora of other RISC chips. But large amounts of Intel's development resources had begun to flow to RISC architecture efforts and there had developed two camps within the company with different views about the future of RISC versus CISC. After a protracted debate, top management, in 1991, decided to reaffirm its commitment to the x86-CISC architecture and to scale down the RISC effort. . . . While some actions may turn out to be helpful, there is also potential danger associated with strategic actions of middle-level managers that diverge from the official strategy. The technical and initial commercial success of the i860 RISC chip as an unplanned stand-alone processor created a strategic dilemma for Intel's top management and extremely strong, eventually divisive, tensions within the organization."[9]

No one would deny that every employee in the organization (not just the salespeople) can contribute to the making of a superior strategy. In fact, given what we know about mental models, it is clear that strategy creation benefits from input from many sources. Nor does anyone deny that since salespeople are indeed closer to the customers, they have a valuable job to do in alerting managers to changing needs or new opportunities. But this does not mean that the process of deciding whom to target as a customer or what to offer as a product is a free-for-all. No, what all this means can be summarized as follows:

1. Everyone in the organization should be actively encouraged to contribute their thoughts, ideas, and opinion as to what strategy the company should adopt.

2. The flow of information from employees on the frontlines back to the firm should be facilitated so that those at the top of the organization know how the strategy is doing and can take quick action to revise the strategy as necessary.

3. People in the field should be given some flexibility to experiment. Nobody puts this better than John Bachmann at Edward Jones when he says, "I give my people the canvas and the paints they have to use. After that, it's up to them to decide what they paint and how. As long as they stay on the canvas and use only the paints I gave them, I'm happy."

4. The decision-making responsibility rests with top management. Abdicating this responsibility in the name of "making strategy democratic" is looking for serious trouble.

One company that is attempting to involve employees as an aid to rather than a substitute for top management decision making is Lan & Spar. The bank has subdivided all 280 of its employees into groups of 10, called decatables. Each decatable has been given a "Strategy Workbook," which is essentially a series of exercises. One exercise, for example, asks employees to think about customers that the bank has lost to competitors and to come up with ideas on how to prevent this from happening in the future. Another exercise asks employees to consider how the Internet might affect business and what the bank should do about it. Yet another exercise asks employees to list the kinds of things taking place in the bank that really upset them. The workbook consists of forty pages of such exercises.

Each decatable is free to meet as often and as long as its members want. Their task is to go through the workbook over a five-month period and record all of the ideas they generate. Each decatable then presents its collection of ideas to the CEO and his top two aides for evaluation. This executive team makes preliminary decisions about which ideas to adopt and which to reject and presents them at a conference attended by all employees, explaining the criteria for their decisions. The conference participants are then encouraged to engage in an open debate with the management team, especially on the ideas that have been rejected.

The process is repeated every year, with variants to prevent the exercise from becoming mechanistic. Of course, every company should find the approach to employee involvement that suits it best, but the approach taken by Lan & Spar is certainly effective. In the last so-called strategy round, more than 300 ideas were presented to the CEO. Not coincidentally, the annual survey of employee attitudes reported record high levels of morale within the company.

This example demonstrates my key point: everyone in the organization should be encouraged to contribute to the decision-making process, but when all is said and done, the decision itself must be made by those at the top.

Questioning Answers: Make It a Habit

The choice of target customers is never final. People should be given the flexibility to experiment with potential new customers and pursue possible new leads. More important, as part of its strategic process, every organization must make it a habit to revisit the question "Who is our customer?" every year. It is only when a company questions what it has always taken for granted that new insights emerge or new customer segments are discovered.

Many companies seem to believe that "new" customer segments present themselves only when new customer needs emerge. New needs certainly do give rise to fresh customer segments, but they are not the only source. Customer needs often remain the same, but customer *priorities* change—for example, customers have continued to need both "warmth" and "style" from their overcoats, but over the past thirty years, the balance has shifted markedly toward style. A company with an eye for such changing priorities (not needs) can carve out a specific and sometimes significant customer niche.[10]

A company may also identify a specific customer segment whose needs are not being met by other competitors. Those competitors may have identified the needs but chosen not to respond. They may have decided, for instance, that the customer segment is not big enough to pursue or that they cannot serve this segment profitably given their existing value chain. If a company can set itself up to serve this niche efficiently, it will have a "new" customer segment at its disposal, not because "new" customer needs have emerged but because it has found a more efficient way to cater to existing ones.

A third way to identify new customer segments is by resegmenting the existing customer base more creatively, putting different customer segments together according to a new logic. Recombination of existing customer segments may also allow a company to "create" a new need and then grow a particular segment.

My purpose here is not to make an exhaustive list of all the possible ways in which a company can identify "new" customer segments. All I want to suggest is that "new" customer segments can be developed in a variety of ways and that the emergence of new customer needs is only one of them. But no company will identify new segments unless it thinks proactively about the question "Who is my customer?" and continually challenges the answer it has come to take for granted.

Inevitably, if a company identifies a "new" customer base, it will start behaving in a way that best satisfies the specific needs of those customers. This behavior will probably differ from that of established competitors serving different customers. By doing what its chosen customer segment needs and wants, the innovating company will appear to its rivals to be "breaking the rules."

Consider again the case of Canon, explored in Chapter 1. There is no question that Canon broke the rules of the game in the copier market. But how did the company come up with all these new ways of competing? Could it be that Canon started out by identifying individuals as a potential customer segment? And it then asked the question, "What do individuals want?" Answer: small personal copiers. And "How can I get these copiers to these individual customers?" Answer: through dealers. Thus we have the Canon strategy, an undeniably innovative one when compared with Xerox's, but in fact nothing more than doing exactly what is needed to satisfy the needs of Canon's chosen customer segment.

Many of the companies that we now consider strategic innovators started out this way. They identified a customer segment (usually but not always the low end of the market) or a niche not being served by competitors. They then designed their products and delivery systems according to the requirements of this customer segment. This source of strategic innovation underpins the success of companies such as Wal-Mart, Canon, Apple, Southwest Airlines, the Body Shop, Texas Instruments (in personal calculators), Lan & Spar Bank, J.C. Penney (back in the early 1900s), *USA Today*, Komatsu, Honda (in motorcycles and cars) and many, many more.

Consider for example Southwest Airlines. At a time when other airlines were using hub-and-spoke systems, CEO Herb Kelleher decided to break the rules. How? By targeting a neglected customer segment: "We wound up with a unique market niche: we are the world's only short-haul, high-frequency, low-fare, point-to-point carrier. . . . We wound up with a market segment that is peculiarly ours, and everything about the airline has been adapted to serving that market segment in the most efficient and economical way possible."[11]

But let's be clear: Choosing a "niche" is not in itself strategic innovation. To qualify as strategic innovation, the chosen niche must grow to become the dominant market, such that *this* way of playing the game becomes *the* way to play the game. It is the choice of the "right" niche that qualifies as strategic innovation.

Therefore, strategic innovators appear to emerge in the following manner. At a given time, the mass market is served by a number of competitors. For whatever reason, a company spots a segment or niche and goes after it. Existing competitors take no umbrage with the move because it is not really taking customers away from them (that is, they still control the mass market). Given the way the company with the new niche plays the game, the other players may not even perceive it as a competitor. Then suddenly the niche grows, and before you know it this niche company emerges as the new market leader. Now all other competitors take notice and search frantically for a way to respond. Academics the world over label this company a maverick competitor that won big time by breaking the rules. This scenario is a perfect fit with the success stories of companies like Canon, Apple, Southwest Airlines, Wal-Mart, Dell, Snapple, CNN, MTV, and Nucor, among others.

Each of these companies chose a specific market niche that exploded. But what does it mean to say that a niche grew to become the new mass market? It means something that had been important to only a few people has now become important to almost everyone. (An example would be concern for the environment, a niche that grew in the 1980s along with the fortunes of the environmentally conscious Body Shop). How did this happen? Either the need was already there and a company was lucky or quick enough to catch the wave just as it began to rise, or the company helped grow this need so as to exploit it. Thus, the important thing is to pick the "right" niche.[12]

How do strategic innovators pick the "right" niche? There is no magic formula. Choosing the right niche requires a deep understanding of customer needs and priorities and the ways these are likely to change in the future. It also requires the courage (most vividly seen in entrepreneurs) to take the risk of pursuing what appears to be a promising customer segment but which may very well turn out to be a dead end.

What Is It That We Sell to Our Customers?

The second strategic decision a company must make concerns what products or services to offer its customers. Just as a company can't target every conceivable customer, it can't offer every product or service to everyone. It has to focus. Trying to offer everything to everybody gets you nobody.

This point is made forcibly by Paul Cook, the founder of Ray-chem Corporation. The company is in the business of supplying technology-intensive products to industrial customers in industries such as aerospace, autos, telecommunications, and utilities. According to Cook:

> I think [a] more powerful way to compete is to avoid competition alto-gether. The best way to avoid competition is to sell products that rivals can't touch. When we started Raychem, the last thing we wanted to do was make products that giants like GE or Du Pont would also be inter-ested in making. We made sure to select products that would not be of interest to large companies. We selected products that could be cus-tomized, that we could make in many varieties—different sizes, differ-ent thicknesses, different colors. We wanted products that were more, not less, complicated to design and build. We wanted products with small potential annual revenues compared with the total size of the company, and we wanted lots of them. After 33 successful years, I still have trouble pushing that vision inside Raychem; people struggle against it all the time. . . . People argue that it would be much easier, that we would grow more quickly, if we put less inventive content in our products and went for bigger markets. That's not my idea of a smart way to grow a business.[13]

The key question, then, is: "Of all the possible products (or ser-vices) your company could offer, which ones should it focus on?" Most people assume this to be a no-brainer: just offer the customer what that customer wants. How many times have you heard peo-ple say, "The customer is king" or "Success in business comes from giving the customer what the customer really wants"? A few exam-ples should suffice to debunk this myth.

The next time you visit your doctor, explain that you are her customer, that, as everybody knows, "the customer is always right," and that "she should give the customer what the customer really wants." Follow this opening statement with a request to pur-chase some cocaine or morphine from her. Chances are, she will refuse to sell you what you really want. Why? Is this a sign that your doctor is not "customer oriented"?

Consider another example: Some years ago, the London Business School was approached by a leading British newspaper company with a proposal that the two combine forces and start offering short, one- or two-day courses on "hot" managerial issues (such as process reengineering, empowerment, benchmarking, and the like) to senior executives. This was (and still is) a growth market. The school would be responsible for designing and delivering the courses, while the newspaper company would take on the task of marketing them. Despite the apparent attractiveness of this proposal, the school turned it down. Why? Does this show that the London Business School is neither opportunistic nor customer focused?

The point here is that while our customers' wants or needs can help us identify what we *could* be offering, we must apply many more criteria before deciding what we *should* be offering. Your doctor is not going to prescribe cocaine because it is illegal. The London Business School does not want to offer short executive courses on hot managerial topics because it does not believe it has the competencies to be the best provider of these products. Different criteria are applied to decide what to offer and what not to offer. Just because a customer wants or needs something, it does not necessarily mean that you should be the one providing it.

This discussion suggests that, as in the case of deciding who to target as customer, a company can decide what products or services to offer by considering two separate issues (see Exhibit 3-3).

Exhibit 3-3   Deciding on the "What"

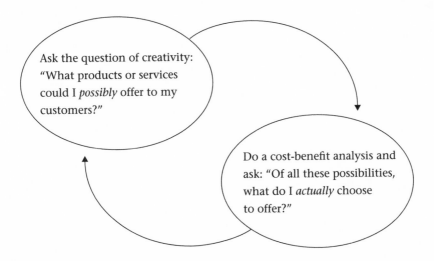

1. First, the company should identify all possible products it *could* be offering. Starting from a list of new or latent customer needs, it has to decide what products might satisfy them. This is a process that requires creativity. The potential for major strategic innovation lies at this point, especially if you aggressively question preconceived notions about what you are really offering to customers. As shown in Exhibit 3-4 and discussed below, a company can use a variety of tactics to identify possible new products.

2. Second, the company has to decide which of these potential products it will *actually* offer. To do this, it must draw up a set of criteria for evaluating all possible products and then select those which meet its criteria. This implies that every company must have a list of criteria that guides its decisions about what products to offer and what products to pass on. For example, Hewitt Associates is always looking at new products and services that might "contribute to our employees' satisfaction and fun, that can be profitable, that the customer needs, that are within the field of human relations, and that [can build] on our core competencies."

Again, as is the case in deciding what customers to target, the thinking process involved in determining what products or services to sell is not (and should not be) linear. You do not complete the first step and then move on to the second. You could (and you should) also begin your thinking with the second step and then move on to the first. This means that you could first ask the question: "What products could I possibly offer?" and then evaluate all the ideas generated to decide what actually to offer. Alternatively, you could begin by developing a list of criteria for evaluating new product ideas. Then you could ask the question: "Given these criteria, what would be good products for me to be offering?" Creativity is enhanced by forcing the mind to start its thinking at different points.

Identifying Possible Products

As Exhibit 3-4 shows, a company can identify new product ideas in a number of ways. The obvious way, of course, is to ask the customer. While doing so is absolutely necessary, it is crucial to realize that simply asking the customer (or monitoring customer changes) usually will not lead to new products. There are many reasons for this,[14] but key is the fact that customers can tell you only about their perceived needs and wants. Determining what the company has to do to meet them requires making an admittedly difficult creative leap.

Consider, for example, the case of a German company that manufactures coffee percolators.[15] When it asked its customers what they wanted from their percolators, they gave the obvious response: "good-quality coffee." What the percolator manufacturer needed to do to meet that stated need, however, was not so obvious. Most of the time, customer needs or changing customer behaviors are at one level quite apparent. But translating the underlying need into innovative products or services is a different matter entirely.

Asking the customer can be an important source of new product ideas, but it should be obvious that this is but one source of innovation. Another useful way to identify new products or services is

---

Exhibit 3-4   How to Identify New Products or Services

- Ask the customer.

- Understand your customer's business.

- Identify trends in the market.

- Benchmark inside or outside the industry.

- Seek the advice of external experts.

- Experiment with new product ideas.

- Seek feedback from suppliers, customers, and distributors.

- Build on your core competencies to develop new products that surprise the customer.

- Involve everybody in the organization in generating new product ideas.

- Apply what you learned from diversification.

---

to develop a deep understanding of your customer's business and the way in which your customer satisfies *its* customers' needs. Doing so allows you to think ahead of the customer and discover new services to provide even before the customer is aware of needing them. The question is, "How do you get a better understanding of your customers' business?" Several tactics can be used: talk to your customer's customers, competitors, employees, and suppliers; understand your customer's value chain; become partners with your customer by developing a close working relationship; monitor new entrants into your customers' business; and so on.

Outside benchmarking can also be a source of new trends and new products. For example, Hanes originated its innovative idea to distribute women's pantyhose through supermarkets when in 1968, Robert Elberson, president of the Hanes hosiery division, noticed that a West German pantyhose manufacturer had introduced its line (Lady Brevoni) to supermarkets in several metropolitan areas in the eastern United States. Similarly, the Kresge Co. transformed itself into Kmart in the late 1950s after its president, Harry Cunningham, spent two years studying Korvette, the nation's most successful discount store chain and the firm that inaugurated the U.S. discounting revolution in the 1950s.

Another tactic is to experiment with new products until you hit upon a latent need. For example, more than 1,000 new soft drinks appear annually in Japan, with only 1 percent actually making it through the year.[16] The moral is that you will not create a new niche or discover a latent consumer need unless you try. You need to do "expeditionary marketing": placing many small bets in quick succession, learning and adjusting as you go along, hoping that you'll make good on one of them.[17]

Opportunities for new product ideas may also come up in the normal course of doing business. The required ingredients are an open mind, the willingness to experiment, and the capacity to apply the resulting knowledge to product development. Sometimes what begins as an incremental, step-by-step approach to improving a product or service can end up transforming the business altogether.

Consider the case of Vons, a grocery chain on the West Coast. Professor William Davidson, who studied the company, reported:

They were among the first to install scanners at the checkout counter. Initially, their only goals were to cut labor costs and better manage inventory. Well, they got so focused on speeding up the checkout transaction that they started to address the sources of delay. One was payment by check, so Vons became, I believe, the first grocery chain to offer a check-writing-privilege card that you could just swipe [through a machine] at the counter for automatic approval. Eventually they realized that this technology could capture the identity of their customers and what they were buying. So Vons started to use the data in targeted ways, and they're now a major force in the direct-marketing information-services business. When you swipe that card, you get special discounts, credits toward free prizes, and more.[18]

Yet another source of new product ideas can be company employees. These people know the products well and interact with customers often. They have a wealth of information that is waiting to be tapped. However, as I explain in Chapter 6, the company has to create the right organizational environment if this kind of innovation is to take root.

Becoming a more customer-oriented company can clearly help a company to identify new products and services. But is that enough? Did Sony really come up with the walkman by focusing on the customer? Did Yamaha develop its electronic pianos as a result of a deeper understanding of its customers? Although the answer to both of these questions may be yes, this line of questioning points to another possible source of new products: building on the organization's existing core competencies.[19]

A fascinating example of this principle is provided by 3M. In 1995, 3M sold close to $1 billion in microreplication products, ranging from "smart" adhesives to liquid-crystal-display film. These products stem from a single technology, which was first used in the lens of an overhead projector thirty years before. According to the inventor of this first microreplication product, Roger Appeldorn, no one planned for any of the products that followed: "We didn't sit down and say, 'Microreplication is the next thing to do; let's go do it.' It doesn't work this way. It evolved. It reached a critical mass. And it suddenly proliferated."[20]

Leveraging existing core competencies is certainly one way to create new products and new ways of competing. But it is not enough. To be successful in the long term, companies need to use their competencies in a dynamic way to generate knowledge that will allow them to create new competitive advantages on a continuing basis. Competition is a never-ending game; any advantage will eventually be eroded unless the firm uses every available opportunity to develop new ones.

This is especially the case for companies that have experimented with diversification. By competing in different markets, diversified firms gain access to new knowledge and experiences that are unavailable to other firms. If they use this new knowledge effectively, they should be able to develop new assets and capabilities faster and more economically than their nondiversified competitors. Herein lies the most important—and most overlooked—benefit of diversification: it is a great learning experience and an invaluable source of new knowledge. Firms that take advantage of this benefit will use their diversification as a springboard for growth.

The learning that a firm accumulates from its diversification moves can be put to use in three distinct ways. First, it can be used to *improve* the firm's operations in a new product market. For example, when Canon diversified from cameras to copiers, its camera division had already developed a set of competencies, such as the knowledge of how to increase the effectiveness of a dealer network, how to develop new products combining optics and electronics, and how to squeeze more productivity out of high-volume assembly lines. All this knowledge is directly applicable to the copier business, in which the processes of improving dealer effectiveness, accelerating product development, and increasing assembly-line productivity are similar to those in the camera business. As a result, Canon was able to apply its accumulated knowledge in the camera business to improve the quality of its processes in the copier business (and vice versa).

A firm can also use its learning from diversification to *create* new capabilities in a new market faster or at a lower cost than its competitors can. In the course of operating in the copier business, Canon learned new skills, such as how to build a marketing organization targeted to business (rather than personal buyers) and the knowledge of developing and manufacturing a reliable electrostatic printing engine. Canon can use this knowledge to diversify into the laser printer business much more quickly and cheaply than a firm that is trying to diversify from scratch (something which it has in fact now done). It can also use this knowledge to avoid making the costly mistakes that novices tend to make when entering a brand new business.

Finally, a firm can use its learning from diversification by *capitalizing on synchronicity*. In creating the capabilities required to support the design, manufacture, and service of the more sophisticated electronics demanded by the laser printer business, Canon also developed new competencies that could be used to improve its photocopier business. Alternatively, combining the competencies developed in its photocopier and laser printer businesses may have helped the company to quickly and cheaply build the capabilities required to succeed in a fourth market: that for plain paper facsimiles.

Thus, the long-run value of diversification lies not so much in exploiting existing core competencies as in allowing the corporation to learn new things and expand its current capabilities more efficiently and more quickly than its competitors can. In a dynamic world, only those firms which are able to build new capabilities faster and more cheaply than their competitors will earn superior returns over time. By transferring core competencies between its divisions, a corporation can accelerate the rate and lower the cost at which it accumulates new capabilities. Successful diversifiers will be those which first recognize the importance of this "learning" benefit of diversification and then put into place structures and processes that facilitate and promote such learning throughout the organization.

Numerous other tactics may be used to identify products and services a company *could* be offering to customers. Once the list of possibilities is assembled, the next step is to select the right ones. Each new product idea must be evaluated according to a set of criteria before the decision to offer it is made.

Identifying Selection Criteria

Product ideas need to be screened on a cost-benefit basis. For each new product idea, a company must ask, "How much will it cost me to make this product and how much can I charge for it?" The relative benefits (that is, price) and costs of a proposed product will be determined not only by what the customer really needs or wants (and is therefore willing to pay) but also by the company's own competencies and capabilities. This point is all too often overlooked.

Ideally, a company will want to focus on "profitable," high-margin products. These must be products that the customer really wants and is therefore ready to pay out big margins to get them. But remember: these high-margin products are exactly those which your competitors will also want to offer. If all of these companies offer the customer the same kind of products, how long will the margins on them remain high?

Clearly, in deciding what products to offer, you need to look beyond the intrinsic characteristics of the product. You must also look at your unique bundle of assets and capabilities and determine whether, given these competencies, you have any competitive advantage in offering a particular product to a customer. At the end of the day, a good product for your company is one that the customer really wants *and* that your company has an advantage in offering. It is the combination of these two factors that allows you to earn a fat margin on a product.

Different companies have different competencies, so a good product for a competitor to be offering may not be a good product for your company to be offering. Your task is to identify products that will allow you to maximize the impact of your unique capabilities relative to competitors. Since advantages get eroded over time, you should always be searching for new products and services to offer. If a competitor imitates an offering, you needn't necessarily drop the product and move onto something else; you need it just to stay level with that competitor. But if you want to beat the competition you must continually come up with new products and services. Continual innovation is the only solution.

Questioning Answers

Just as it is imperative to continually question the "rightness" of existing customers, it is imperative for a company to continually question the "rightness" of existing products and services. A product exists to satisfy certain customer needs. A company must therefore be on the lookout for changing customer needs that might make its product obsolete. The question "What are we really offering the customer?" must be raised and answered continually. Through such questioning, a company may be the first to identify new or changing customer needs and so become the first to develop new products that satisfy the new needs.

For example, Canon's strategic innovation in copiers could have arisen from the observation that users do not like waiting in line to use a central copier.[21] To meet this implied need, Canon developed the idea of a personal photocopier, which led to the development of the home market for copiers. Canon was able to create a new market because it was the first to identify the customers' changing preferences. The question is: "How did Canon identify the customers' changing needs or priorities and, more important, how did it move from the observation that people don't like standing in line to developing the personal copier?"

All the tactics identified earlier in this section (questioning the customer, thinking ahead of the customer, using expeditionary marketing, leveraging competencies to develop products that the customer hasn't thought of, and so on) can and should help a company identify changing needs and come up with new product ideas. But how *else* can a company improve the odds that it will think creatively about the "what"?[22]

As with the consideration of "who," one way is to question existing mental models about what is really being offered to customers. Another way of enhancing creativity at this stage is to begin your thinking at different "starting points." Many companies seem to believe that the choice of customers automatically leads them to the choice of products and services they should be offering. This may be so, but from the perspective of strategic innovation, it is also wise to think of the "what" first and then think of who to target. Instead of saying "These are my customers so let's identify what they want so I can offer it to them," try reversing the logic: "Based on my core competencies, these are the products or services that I want to offer; let's think about who would want to buy them."

Summary

1. The decisions made about "who" the company will sell to and "what" it will sell are strategic decisions that define the parameters within which a company will operate. In so doing, they also define the terrain the company will not fight for: the customers it will *not* pursue, the investments it will *not* finance, the competitors it will *not* respond to. Consequently, these decisions can be very painful to make and are often preceded by internal debates, disagreements, and politicking. But in the end they must be made to prevent the company from expending its limited resources with no clear focus or direction.

2. The decisions made about "who" and "what" involve two different questions. First is a creativity question: "Who could I possibly target or what could I possibly offer my customers?" Second is an accounting question: "Of all these possibilities, who do I actually target and what do I actually offer my customers?" It is important not to confuse these two questions.

3. The decisions made about customers or products and services are not cast in concrete. The company should continually revisit these decisions. Opportunities should not be ignored, and the company must always be on the alert to capture another customer segment or to offer an additional product if the opportunity arises. But being opportunistic does not mean refraining from making choices. Rather, it means that the company has, first and foremost, decided where to spend its money, managerial attention, and marketing efforts, yet it leaves some room for experimentation on the periphery. Chief executives who resist making these tough decisions in the name of "flexibility," "democracy," or "opportunism" are abdicating one of their most crucial responsibilities. Their companies resemble a rudderless ship drifting in the ocean with no clear direction, justifying its sorry state by arguing that the ocean is full of treasure islands, and moving in just one direction would mean missing most of them. In their desire not to miss any treasure island, they end up missing all of them.

4

Decide How You
Will Play the Game

I believe we have a sustainable competitive advantage. This does not stem from any one thing we do. Rather, it is based on the system that we have built—the numerous things we carry out on a daily basis which reinforce each other and form a mosaic which is recognizably different to our customers. Our advantage stems from this reinforcing mosaic, not one or two things.

—John Bachmann, Managing Principal, Edward Jones

Let them come and benchmark us. We are not afraid. At best, what they'll do is copy one or two of our best practices. But can they copy the whole system? I doubt it.

—Peter Schou, CEO, Lan & Spar Bank

After targeting the "right" customers (who) and determining the "right" products or services (what), a company is then faced with the question of how—how to play the game, how to do business, how to get the right products to the right customers. How does the company get from here to there—where it wants to be?

Deciding on the "how" is tantamount to designing the firm's value chain of activities—from the purchase of raw materials to the manufacture and sale of the final products and services to the targeted customers. In addressing the question of how, the firm must (re)develop each and every one of its functional policies: from the four Ps of marketing (price, place, promotion, and product) to the technology used in the factory, from how much debt to bear to what kind of human resource policies to promote, from what work to do in-house to what work to subcontract to outsiders.

Designing an optimal value chain and developing functional policies are obviously important issues for every firm. However, they are not the real core of strategy. In fact, determining what activities to pursue is relatively easy and straightforward—all one has to do is to ask: "Given the market I am in, what are the key factors of success? What should I be doing to be successful?" The answers to these kinds of questions should produce a precise (and often lengthy) list of activities to pursue. However, strategy involves much more than the development of individual activities. Strategy is all about *combining* these activities into a *system* that creates the requisite *fit* between the needs of the environment and the actions taken by the company.[1] Strategy will be successful if it creates a well-balanced system of activities that support and reinforce each other and allow the firm to achieve fit with its environment.

At the same time, however, it must be kept in mind that the "fitness"—between what the company does and what the environment requires—has often been dismissed as static. "What happens when the environment changes?" people ask. In such a case, the argument goes, companies that created a good fit with the old environment will, like dinosaurs, perish in the new environment. While this argument has merit, it bears careful interpretation. The point to take away is not that a company should hesitate to achieve fit with its environment but that a company needs to create the requisite fit with its current environment while remaining flexible enough to respond to changes in this environment.[2] As I describe below, this can be achieved in a number of ways.

In this chapter we will look at how a company can develop a system of reinforcing activities to achieve fit with its environment. We will also look at the nature of this fit, which should be dynamic enough both to accommodate the needs of the current environment and respond to changes in this environment.

Creating a Reinforcing System of Activities

Imagine the McDonald's corporation at a time when top management is trying to decide how to diversify. Three businesses have made the short list:

1. frozen foods

2. theme parks

3. photo processing

Which business would allow McDonald's to maximize the value of its core competencies? In a series of experiments at London Business School, we presented this scenario to several groups of senior executives and asked them to decide on behalf of McDonald's.[3] Their answers are revealing.

About 40 percent of the executives suggested that McDonald's, with its competencies in picking good real estate locations and offering family entertainment, should expand into the theme park business. However, 30 percent of the executives singled out McDonald's competencies in offering products of consistent quality with great efficiency. This suggested to them that the photo processing business would be the best match for McDonald's. This choice also has the advantage of allowing the company to exploit its existing distribution outlets. Finally, the remaining 30 percent recommended diversification into the frozen food business because that business could be built on McDonald's competencies in food retailing, supplier relationships, and distribution.

Notice first that through this exercise McDonald's core competencies have in effect been identified as:

- picking good real estate locations

- providing family entertainment

- providing quick service

- providing consistency in product offering

- having an excellent distribution network

- having knowledge of the food business

- having knowledge of food retailing

- having good supplier relationships

Also notice that McDonald's success rests on quite a few activities. One or two cannot be singled out—all of them are important, and trying to find "the one" source of McDonald's success misses the point completely. Finally, notice that the consideration of diversification "forces" the break-up of these core competencies: the first two can be separated out and applied to the theme-park business, the next three to the photo processing business, and the last three to the frozen food business. Is there something wrong with this way of thinking?

First, it is inward-looking and myopic. (Yes, McDonald's could exploit its distribution and supplier competencies in the frozen food business, but will this be enough to make it a success in that business?) Still worse, it denies the existence of synergies—the interaction of the competencies that makes the combined whole greater than its separated parts. Breaking up the competencies into new combinations to support other businesses may in fact destroy some of their worth. A core competence in isolation may not be as valuable as it is when coupled with other competencies.

The question to keep in mind is the following: "Is this competence or activity as important to have in isolation as in combination with all the other activities?" The importance of asking this question becomes apparent when we consider the reason for McDonald's success in the fast-food business. It can be attributed to two factors:

1. The fit and balance among all of these competencies and activities such that they support and reinforce one another.

2. The fit between this constellation of competencies and activities and the requirements of the fast-food market. In effect, McDonald's is a smooth-running machine whose competencies and activities allow it to do exactly what is needed in this market. For a potential competitor to imitate McDonald's, that competitor must imitate every single one of McDonald's practices *and* combine them into a balanced system just as McDonald's has done. Thus, the greater the number of activities that make up the McDonald's "system," and the more closely these activities are linked, the more difficult it is for a potential competitor to imitate McDonald's suc-

cess (and, therefore, the more likely it is that McDonald's will be able to sustain its advantage.)[4]

Thus the very act of unbundling McDonald's competencies so as to apply them in different combinations in different markets actually destroys their "fitness" and may also weaken the value of the individual competencies. What makes McDonald's successful is not the individual competencies but the uniqueness of their combination. Whether a different combination of competencies will allow McDonald's to succeed in a different market depends on how effectively this new combination of competencies fits both within the company and within the new market.

The McDonald's example illustrates what a company should aim for in constructing its strategy: to arrange the individual activities it needs to be successful into a jigsaw puzzle. The first part of this task—determining what activities a firm must carry out—is easy. The difficult part is putting all the activities together so that they support and reinforce each other. Equally difficult is the task of ensuring that this fragile jigsaw does not come apart under stress as time goes by.

The Case of People Express

The importance of conceptualizing the company as a combination of activities cannot be overemphasized. From this perspective, a firm is a complex system of interrelated and interdependent activities, each one affecting the other: decisions and actions in one part of the business affect other parts, directly or indirectly. Unless you take a holistic, big-picture approach in designing the activities of your company, your efforts will backfire. Even if each individual activity is optimally crafted, the whole may still suffer unless you take interdependencies into consideration. *The numerous local optima almost always undermine the global optimum.*

Consider, for example, the case of People Express, an airline created in 1980 by Don Burr to compete in the eastern part of the United States as a low-cost, no-frills operation. The company achieved tremendous growth and success in the first half of the 1980s only to go bankrupt and be acquired by Texas Air in 1986.

From the very beginning, Don Burr had determined that People's success would depend on its ability to provide frequent flights at very low prices. For example, whereas other competitors charged $123 on the Newark-to-Pittsburgh route, People entered that market with a $19 fare in April 1982. But low fares did not mean poor quality. Burr positioned People to offer no-frills flights but with superior customer service. These three goals (cheap, frequent, good-quality flights) were listed on People's application for a flying certificate to the Civil Aeronautics Board in 1980. Don Burr and his management team set about to achieve them by putting a number of initiatives to work.

People Express made headlines in the early 1980s for its rock-bottom prices. How did it manage this? Low labor costs were one factor that made these low prices possible. To keep labor costs low, Burr did not resort to low salaries but tried instead to maintain an extremely productive workforce. To create and maintain high labor productivity, Burr created a culture in which everyone was treated equally and people were encouraged to share ideas, help each other, and work together. In addition, Burr gave each employee share options in the company. This meant that as long as the company grew, the stock price increased and employees benefited. Of course, this practice inevitably put pressure on the company to grow, which led to the purchase of additional planes and the hiring of new people.

Along with low prices, People offered frequent flights. To provide this service, Burr centered company operations in the densely populated New York–Newark area, with service at the underutilized, uncongested, highly accessible Newark international airport. Also helping People keep up the pace was its practice of limiting the time its planes spent grounded at the gate. The company was able to keep gate time down in part because of the company's flexible labor force, which was willing to do whatever it took to get the planes in the air quickly, and in part because of such practices as ticketing onboard, limiting baggage handling, and subcontracting plane maintenance.

Notice that no single factor can be separated out as the reason for People's initial success. The success of the company rested on an entire series of activities rather than one or two. Exhibit 4-1

Exhibit 4-1 The People Express Growth Machine: A System of Reinforcing Activities

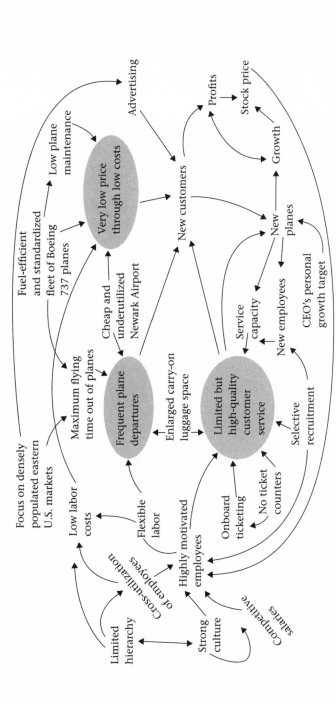

Source: This diagram was created by John Morecroft and is published with his permission. It appears in J. D. W. Morecroft, *People Express—Managing a Dynamic Resource System* (software and slidepack), Educational Document ED-0002-A, System Dynamics Group, Decision Technology Centre, London Business School, January 1996.

shows what is called a causal loop diagram of the many activities People engaged in: use of cheap planes, hiring and support of a highly motivated and productive labor force, practice of time-efficient efforts at airport gates, support of a democratic, open culture, efficient utilization of planes, and more. It should also be noted—and this is evident in the diagram—that all of the activities undertaken by People Express were interconnected. Decisions made in one part of the system eventually affected other parts of the system. For example, the operation manager's decision to purchase more planes would eventually influence the growth rate of the company, which would in turn influence the productivity of the employees, and eventually the quality of the service. This, in turn, would influence the number of new passengers the airline would attract (and the number of existing passengers it retained), which would in turn influence the number of airplanes the company needed to buy (or to sell).

Every business has similar interdependencies. But because it is very difficult for people inside the company (as well as outside) to comprehend all the complexity that is embedded within it, they tend to focus on one or two aspects of the system and try to optimize these subsystems independently.[5] For example, when confronted with declining revenues, People Express might have tried to attract more passengers by increasing its advertising, ignoring the fact that the real problem was perhaps a deterioration in the quality of service provided by newly hired, inadequately trained employees. By stepping up its advertising, People might have inadvertently worsened its problem by raising customer expectations and failing to meet them, thus losing more customers at a faster rate!

By trying to optimize subsystems independently, managers ignore the interdependencies in the system and thereby make matters worse. Since it takes time for the effect of such actions to surface, it's also very hard to see that more often than not, we are the source of the problem. When the long-term effects of these short-sighted actions hit home, the tendency is to blame other people or outside factors.

Conceptualizing the firm as a complex system of interrelated activities is half the battle. An experienced management team can, collectively, describe the operating structure of the business and draw a "diagram" of their business very much like the People Express diagram in Exhibit 4-1. These causal loop diagrams are a powerful graphic tool that can plainly show the interconnectedness of a business. The purpose of creating such a diagram is not to capture all the company's complexity, to get the diagram exactly "right," or to use it to predict the future. Rather, it's purpose is to help top management gain insight. The insight comes when managers challenge the content of the diagram, talk with one another about their assumptions and beliefs, and then revise the diagram accordingly. Learning is the natural consequence of building a consensus about how their business system really works.[6]

How to Put a System Together

In designing the company's system of activities, managers must bear four principles in mind. First, the individual activities you choose to undertake must be the ones that are demanded by the market. For example, there is no sense in developing an extensive network of dealers if you can distribute your product more effectively through the Internet. Similarly, there is no point in building or leveraging your core competencies in channel management if customers are increasingly buying direct from the market. The point is simple: in deciding what activities to perform (or what competencies to leverage), you must always start with an analysis of the market. The goal is to the identify activities that will give you "fit" with what the market requires.

Second, the activities you decide to perform must fit together (recall the jigsaw). For example, manufacturing must be able to make the products that marketing is promoting. Similarly, you cannot aim to exploit synergies across your subsidiaries (by, for example, transferring key people) without developing incentive systems to encourage such behavior. Again, the point here is simple: the internal fit between activities is as important as the collective fit these activities achieve with the market.

Third, these activities must also be in *balance* with one another. Consider, for example, what happens as a firm grows. If you increase the firm's manufacturing capacity without increasing its sales and marketing capacity, you will end up with excessive inventories.

Similarly, if you increase the sales and marketing capacity without increasing the production capacity, you will end up with a lot of unserved (and dissatisfied) customers. The lesson is not to invest in one or the other but to invest in both simultaneously to maintain a balance among these activities over time.

The difficulty of achieving and maintaining balance among activities over time should not be underestimated. Losing it has been the undoing of many companies. Consider, for example, Southwest Airlines, which is often hailed as a truly innovative company that took on the giants and succeeded. Of the many activities that underpin Southwest's success story, we could point to the following: a flat organizational structure that encourages open communication; the practice of transferring and cross-utilizing staff in different areas of the organization, which promotes communication, exchange of knowledge, and the development of people who see "the big picture"; the ability to hire high-quality staff, which leads to high productivity; a cooperative and friendly culture that promotes teamwork; its high utilization of its people, which leads to high efficiency; and so on. Nobody denies that all of these activities help Southwest succeed in a tough market. Nor can it be denied that things like a flat structure, cross-utilization of people, teamwork, and the like can produce the great benefits listed above.

However, as shown in Exhibit 4-2, each one of these activities can backfire if Southwest is not careful. A flat structure, for example, promotes open communication but also creates a career structure with limited opportunities. Similarly, while high utilization of staff can lead to efficiencies, it can also produce exhausted and stressed people. Teamwork can be motivating and fun, but it may hinder the development of leaders. These negative side effects can, of course, be managed. But trying to maintain the balance so that each one of the activities produces the desired effect without egregious side effects can be enormously difficult.

Fourth and finally, in designing the system of activities, keep in mind that the activities will collectively form an interrelated system. Not only should you pay particular attention to the interrelationships in this system, but you should be aware that the structure of this system will drive behavior. What people in the firm do is conditioned by this underlying structure. Therefore, if you want to

Exhibit 4-2   The Need for Balance in Activities
Example: Southwest Airlines

Southwest Activity	Advantages	Disadvantages
Flat organizational structure	Promotes employee communication	Limits upward career progress
Cross-utilization of employees	Helps everyone see the big picture; promotes transfer of best practices	Discourages development of specialists; can lead to short-term inefficiencies
High-quality staff	Facilitates productivity	Makes recruiting and retaining staff difficult
High utilization of both staff and planes	Promotes efficiency	Leads to exhaustion; causes wear and tear
Teamwork	Helps everyone see the big picture and motivates staff	Limits development of future leaders in the organization
High level of employee stock ownership	Promotes a sense of ownership, which is motivating	Is demotivating when stock price falls
Empowerment of employees	Promotes personal responsibility and can be motivating	Can lead to loss of control and costly mistakes

change behavior, you have to change the structure of the system. I will return to this point in Chapter 6.

Looking at the firm as a system of interrelationships and using causal loop diagrams to depict these interrelationships are ideas that stem from the discipline of systems dynamics. These ideas have not made the inroads they deserve into managerial thinking. It is worthwhile, however, to consider what Peter Senge—one of the influential leaders of the cause—has to say about this:

Frankly, I have been a little concerned about the phrase "systems thinking." What systems thinking is all about is the ability to see through the complexity to what is really essential. Wisdom may be a better term.

The problem with the phrase "systems thinking" is that it tends to connote fighting complexity with complexity. People seem to misinterpret it to say, "the world is becoming increasingly complicated, everything affects everything else, and therefore we have to draw these big complicated pictures." Unfortunately, they then get caught up in producing the world's most complicated diagrams that don't produce any penetrating insights into what is really going on. . . . Drawing a diagram of interdependencies in terms of feedback loops is not systems thinking. It is a diagram. But the diagram can help us get what we are really after: to be able to continuously perceive our world and communicate about it in such a way that the interdependencies become apparent. This is a shift from looking at things to seeing interrelationships, a shift from seeing snapshot A and then snapshot B to seeing them both as well as the process connecting them.[7]

Creating Dynamic Fit

Creating the right fit between what the market needs and what the firm does can backfire if the environment changes and the firm does not respond accordingly. You may be familiar with the story of the frog: when a frog is put in a pot of boiling water, it jumps out; when the same frog is put in a pot of cold water and the water is slowly brought to a boil, the frog stays in the pot and boils to death. Likewise, any organization that does not react to the constant, sometimes subtle changes taking place in its environment will eventually find itself as dead as that frog.

The lesson of this story for the business organization is that it must both create the requisite fit with its current environment *and* remain flexible enough to respond to (or even create) changes in this environment. But what does it mean for a firm to remain flexible? In using the term here, I imply three things: a firm must first be able to identify changes in its environment early enough to respond before it is too late; it must then have the cultural readiness to embrace change and respond to it; and, finally, it must have the requisite skills and competencies to compete in whatever environment emerges after the change. Thus, flexibility has a cultural element (the willingness to change) as well as a competence element (the ability to change). As shown in Exhibit 4-3, this kind of flexibility can be achieved in several ways. I discuss a few of these tactics below.

Exhibit 4-3   Tactics for Achieving Dynamic Fit

- Institutionalize a questioning attitude.

- Create a culture that welcomes change.

- Continuously challenge the organization's unquestioned assumptions and sacred cows.

- Build an early monitoring system to identify turning points in the business.

- Monitor new entrants, niche players, and newly established firms.

- Don't focus too much on existing customers, monitor fringe customers.

- Seek feedback from suppliers, customers, distributors, and employees.

- "Shock" the system into active thinking through the creation of infrequent and unpredictable positive crises.

- Allow "slack" in the system.

- Build a variety of competencies (build core competencies into diverse product lines).

- Develop processes that allow for continual experimentation of ideas.

- Encourage decentralized decision making (within clear parameters set by top management).

Adopt a Questioning Attitude

One of the most powerful ways a firm can instill flexibility in its system is by developing a culture that continually questions the status quo, no matter how successful the firm is. Such a questioning attitude is pervasive in everything the firm does—in a sense, it is institutionalized in the firm's systems and processes. As a result, questioning of the status quo and experimentation "just happen," and nobody really notices because they're nothing out of the ordinary.

What kind of environment promotes this kind of behavior? At the Danish bank Lan & Spar, the CEO knows the name and background of every one of his 250 employees and spends more than

50 percent of his time mixing and talking with them. New ideas from employees are quickly acted on, and small gifts or monetary rewards are given to selected individuals who originated them. At 3M, individuals are "expected" to steal 15 percent of their time to work on unauthorized projects. If a project reaches the stage of new venture, the venture is spun off as a separate division and the entrepreneur is made divisional president. At MCI, people are encouraged to take calculated risks, and top management fosters a culture in which everything is questioned. As a result, whereas in most companies people are afraid to make mistakes, at MCI people are afraid *not* to make mistakes. Note, however, that questioning something doesn't necessarily mean it's not working or needs to change. Questioning it simply means "Let's think about it."

At the Body Shop, every employee has the "ear" of top management through the DODGI Department—the Department of Damn Good Ideas. Every employee with an idea about how to improve the company can call this department and discuss it with senior managers. At ABB, operational decision making has been delegated to more than 5,000 profit centers, and each is empowered to make decisions. At OM Exchange, the first private exchange in Sweden, there is neither a formal hierarchy nor any managerial layers—everyone is an "employee" with the same rights (but different responsibilities). At Leclerc supermarket in France, every store "owner" is free to experiment with new products or formats at will; successes and failures are discussed at regular regional and national meetings.

In short, organizations can choose from an almost unlimited number of tactics and practices to institutionalize innovation and a questioning attitude. In fact, this particular issue is now the most researched topic in the academic literature, and an enormous amount of material exists to help managers institutionalize innovation in their companies. (I won't review that literature in detail here but refer interested readers to some titles as a start.[8]) The compelling question is, if so much is known on how to create a questioning attitude, why do we not see more of this behavior in organizations?

Advising companies to question the way they play the game and to contemplate alternatives is stating the obvious; everyone knows this is what they're supposed to do. It's the business version of the principle that an ounce of prevention is worth a pound of cure; take action *before* the crisis strikes. But while few people (or managers) would disagree with the validity of the principle, few people (or managers) actually abide by it.

To understand why this might be the case, suppose your company goes through the following experience, which is graphically depicted in Exhibit 4-4. The company enjoys a long history of growth and profitability, which culminates at point A, when a sudden change of fortune and financial crisis cause profits to decline. Given this scenario, at what point would you be most likely to undertake serious questioning of the way you operate? If you are at all typical of the majority of companies out there, you would probably start *thinking* about change when profits are already in decline—in the exhibit, at point B; you would probably start *doing* something about it when things get much worse—at point C.

Exhibit 4-4   When to Question the Way We Do Business

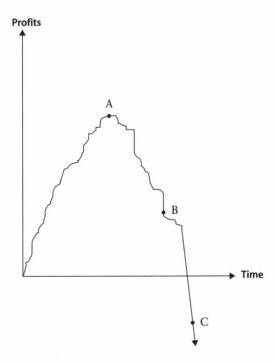

Needless to say, the middle of a crisis is the worst time to execute change. At that point your company lacks the time, resources, and credibility needed to promote a program of long-term change. It is much wiser to think proactively, to consider long-term change when times are good, at their best. You have probably heard this advice a million times: Just because you are successful today doesn't mean you will be successful tomorrow. You should continually question the way you operate. Don't wait until a crisis hits to start contemplating the future.

In fact, the ideal scenario for any company is the pattern of behavior shown in Exhibit 4-5. Well before the company gets into trouble, it actively rejuvenates itself, at point X, allowing it to embark on another growth curve. And just when the new growth curve is about to taper off, the company rejuvenates itself again, at point Y, preparing to embark on yet another growth curve, and so on.[9] (As I will point out later, an organization can identify its position on the curve—and hence decide whether the moment for rejuvenation has arrived—by monitoring both its financial health

Exhibit 4-5   Growth and Rejuvenation

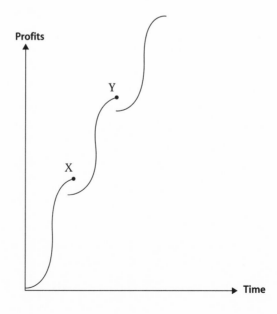

and its strategic health; and it can successfully rejuvenate itself in the manner shown by creating internal "positive crises"—that is, by creating organizational challenges that are then "sold" to the rest of the organization.)

Although this scenario looks utopian, some real-world companies have gone through just such evolutions. Hewlett-Packard made rejuvenating transitions in moving first from instruments to computers, then from minicomputer-based technology to microprocessor-based technology, and finally from computers to desktop publishing. Intel made a similar rejuvenating transition by transforming itself from a DRAM memory company into a microprocessor company. Motorola went from consumer electronics to semiconductors and is now in telecommunications. Johnson & Johnson moved from consumer products to pharmaceuticals. 3M—everybody's favorite company—has changed its business at least three times so far in its history, going from mining to sandpaper to magnetic tapes and so on. Microsoft is in the midst of attempting such a transition as it tries to position itself on the Internet. Likewise, General Electric is in the process of moving heavily into services and out of manufacturing.[10]

Unfortunately, examples such as these are rare. Most companies do not question their way of doing business until a crisis hits. Consider, for example, the experience that Colgate-Palmolive went through in 1994–97. It was only after the 1994 financial results from U.S. operations proved so disastrous that Colgate embarked on a radical restructuring effort. As pointed out by Colgate director, David Johnson: "Sometimes, crisis precedes synthesis. It can take terrible defeat to return with determination and spirit."[11]

The problem, then, is that companies should be questioning the way they do business at point A in Exhibit 4-4, yet most of them don't—no matter how often they are advised to do so. How, then, do strategic innovators succeed in overcoming the inertia of success and fundamentally question the way they do business? I have identified two interrelated approaches:

1. They monitor not only their financial health but also their strategic health—this gives them early warning signals before the crisis actually arrives.

2. They create a positive crisis to galvanize the organization into active thinking. Even more important, because the positive crisis they create usually takes the form of a new challenge for the organization, they take the time to sell the challenge to all of their employees.

Monitor Strategic Health

The reason most companies do not contemplate change at point A is that when they are standing at point A, they see only the upward-climbing line. This suggests to them that they must be doing something right. Why else would profits be soaring? And why doubt that the upward trend will continue?

Even when someone warns them that their profits will take a dip, they ask the natural question: "How do you know what's going to happen?" This is a legitimate question. Surely no one can predict the future, so justifying calls for action now based on what may or may not happen later is dangerous business. Yet strategic innovators seem to have a window on the future; they seem to know a few years before a crisis hits that they must act now to circumvent it. What allows them to predict the future is that they measure not only their *financial* health but also their *strategic* health.

Measuring the financial health of a company is relatively easy. You can examine profitability, revenues, market share, and other financial indicators to get a good sense of how well (or poorly) you are doing. Unfortunately, these financial numbers—though necessary and useful—can be misleading indicators of a company's future. They all measure the past, and, as we all know, the past can sometimes be a very bad predictor of the future. There are countless examples of companies that appear to be very profitable (such as IBM in 1990) yet find themselves in crisis only two or three years down the road. Conversely, many companies that appear to be in financial difficulties (such as IBM in 1994) are really poised for a period of growth and profitability.

A company must go beyond the financial figures to examine its strategic health. *Strategic health* refers to the *future* health of an organization. To monitor its strategic health, a company needs to find a way to measure it. Such measures of strategic health are like early warning systems: they alert you to the signs of crisis two or three years before the crisis is likely to arrive, making it possible to take corrective action.[12] (Whether a company takes advantage of these early warnings is another matter.)

Consider, for example, the case of Boddington Group PLC, discussed in Chapter 2. In 1989, when Denis Cassidy became CEO and chairman, he decided to strategically reorient the company, moving it away from the brewing of beer into "services." Of interest to us here are the reasons for undertaking such a dramatic change in the first place. After all, the company was financially doing quite well. Cassidy rationalized his decision in the following way:

> At the time I took over, the company was still profitable. So, if you only looked at the numbers, there was nothing to worry about. However, when you looked at our business over time, you could tell that something fundamental was happening. For example, consumption of traditional English ale [the traditional lukewarm English "beer" and Boddington's mainstay] went from 85 percent of the population in 1950 to less than 45 percent in 1988. What took its place? Imported beer which could be drunk cold. It's as if the consumer was telling us that our product was not wanted any more. Making the situation even more serious was the fact that the Mergers and Monopolies Commission (MMC) was about to announce its decision on the brewing industry. We all expected that the decision would require big brewers to unbundle their vertical integration by divesting their captive pub operations. These fundamental changes in the industry required action—even though we were still quite profitable.

The story of Boddington highlights a couple of key points. First, notice how this particular manager decided to change his organization's strategy even though his company was financially healthy. What motivated him to act was not the state of his company's financial health but his assessment of its strategic health; he feared that financial problems might surface in the future. As he points out in the above quote, what allowed him to "see" the future were several indicators of strategic health: customer dissatisfaction, structural change in the industry, and deregulation.

Second, notice that it is one thing to pick up on an early warning signal and another thing to decide what to do about it and then do it. This is where strong leadership comes in: being able to envision a different future and then having the courage to abandon the status quo and go for it. These are things that cannot be taught.

The example of Boddington suggests that it *is* possible to measure the strategic health of a company. The list of measures that can be used for this purpose is long (see Exhibit 4-6). Several of the most useful indicators of strategic health are discussed below.

- *Customer satisfaction:* You may have me as a customer today (and that's why you are profitable), but if I am not satisfied with your product or service, you will not have me as a customer tomorrow (and that's why you will face a crisis). Better catch these customers before they leave.

- *Employee morale:* This is an excellent indicator of the "energy level" inside the organization. Unhappy or unmotivated employees usually spell trouble for the future. The roots of internal dissatisfaction need to be identified and the problem rectified.

- *Trends in financial health:* You may be profitable today, making (say) $20 million in profits, but the meaning of that figure will vary depending on what came before. Your assessment of the future ought to be different depending on whether you reached the $20 million level by going up from $10 million in profits two years ago to $13 million last year to this year's $20 million or down from $30 million to $27 million to $20 million.

- *Relative financial health:* Even if your company is very profitable, you should probably worry if your competitors are consistently generating a higher return. You need to compare your company's position with that of its best competitors worldwide.

- *Innovation and new products in the pipeline:* There is no question that Glaxo/Wellcome is very profitable today, but whether it will be profitable tomorrow depends largely on whether it will discover new drugs to replace existing ones—especially as the company's blockbuster drugs (such as Zantac) lose their patent protection.

- *Distributor and supplier feedback:* Distributors and suppliers can provide the company with different perspectives on what's going on in the market; they may indicate areas you should be paying attention to.

- *Changes in the industry and the company's fit with the new environment:* The reason you are profitable today is that you are doing what the market needs. But what if the market is changing? Are you changing with the market, or are you in danger of becoming an institutional dinosaur?

Again, this is not an exhaustive list of the indicators of strategic health that a company can monitor. The important thing to remember is that such indicators do exist and that you should identify those most relevant to your company's business and keep track of them.[13] Only then can you argue that you are assessing the firm's present position in a balanced way. If everyone in the organization is expected to monitor the firm's strategic health, so

Exhibit 4-6   Evaluating Performance: Financial Health and Strategic Health

Strategic Health
- Customer satisfaction
- Customer loyalty
- Market share
- Employee morale
- Staff turnover
- Employee communication
- Trends in financial health
- Financial health relative to best competitors
- Innovation and new products in the pipeline
- Relative manufacturing cost
- Product quality
- Manufacturing flexibility
- Quality of management team
- Distributor and supplier feedback
- Strength of company culture
- Changes in the industry and the company's fit with the new environment

Financial Health
- Profits
- Cashflow
- Shareholder value
- Growth rates

much the better. As Dale Gifford, CEO of Hewitt Associates, points out:

> At Hewitt, we are always watching for shifts in the needs and wants of our clients because there are always early warning signals. We have thousands of associates doing this naturally as part of their role—that is, our people talking with clients and participating in forums. In order to continue being successful, we need to be a little bit nervous, always looking for signals, never taking our success for granted.

Most companies do not bother collecting information on their strategic health. But even the few that do examine some of these indicators (such as customer satisfaction or employee morale) attempt it perhaps every six months or every year. Yet indicators of financial health are monitored every day. Why such imbalance in emphasis? The information systems of the modern corporation have been explicitly developed to allow us to monitor our financial health almost daily—and yet the monitoring of strategic health, even on a yearly basis, requires a special effort. Again, why such an imbalance? Finally, financial results that fall below expectations usually lead to action. When was the last time *your* organization acted on the information contained in an indicator of strategic health?

To assess its present position correctly, an organization has to go beyond financial numbers. It has to examine its strategic health. It must therefore develop appropriate measures of strategic health and use its information systems to collect the data needed to calculate these measures on a regular basis. Only by monitoring these indicators of strategic health can it hope to identify the need for change before a financial crisis hits.

To sum up: Successful companies are able to question the status quo even when they are financially successful (point A in Exhibit 4-4). One tactic they use to do this is to monitor not only their financial health but also their strategic health. Doing so gives them an early warning that allows them to question things before a crisis hits.

Create Positive Crises

Another tactic strategic innovators use to overcome the inertia of success and to instill flexibility is to "shock" the system into active thinking. What innovators seem to know is that it does not matter how actively you question your way of doing things or how much you encourage this kind of behavior in the organization. Eventually, the system will reach a stage of "blissful" stability, characterized by self-satisfaction, overconfidence or even arrogance, a strong but monolithic culture, a strong institutional memory that allows the company to operate on automatic pilot, and strong internal political coalitions. Inevitably, success will breed unyielding mental models that in turn produce passive thinking. These things will happen no matter how successfully you have institutionalized a questioning attitude. Every few years, then, something must happen to shock and destabilize the system all over again. Note that this argument is contrary to the current accepted wisdom, which encourages companies to aim for continuous improvements. Here the argument is for periodic, sudden jolts.

Successful innovators excel at stirring things up. They are not afraid to destabilize a smoothly running machine—and to do so periodically—because no one can know in advance exactly when the system will need this jolt. Witness, for example, what Jack Welch has done at General Electric over the past twenty years. In the early 1980s, he took GE through a massive and painful restructuring program, a challenge that earned him the nickname Neutron Jack. The restructuring was a success, transforming GE into one of the most admired corporations in the country during the 1990s. Then, in late 1997, just when GE was posting record operating margins of 14.5 percent and a stellar 25 percent-plus annual return on equity, Welch announced a new massive restructuring program.

How can a company create "shocks" to the system? One powerful way, as the GE example shows, is to develop *positive crises*. A positive crisis is nothing more than a stretching and challenging new goal that has been sold throughout the organization.

The notion that stretching goals can be good for an organization is not new.[14] And, as most senior managers know, it has lately become very popular for organizations to include them in their mission statements. The problem is that most of these statements are not worth the paper they were written on.

Why might that be the case? Because a stretching goal is useless unless people buy into it; and if people are going to buy into anything, an effort must be made to sell it to them. Now ask yourself: What are the chances that a simple statement—however sexy it sounds—will, by itself, generate buy-in? The answer is zero. No matter how grand or appealing the statement, if time and effort have not been devoted to selling the idea to employees, it will fail to excite them. The crucial part is selling it to every employee. A challenge that employees do not embrace will lead to cynicism, negative feelings, and lack of motivation. Conversely, a positive crisis generates passion, enthusiasm, and energy on the part of employees toward the firm and what it is trying to achieve.

Successful innovators create positive crises not by denying how well their organization is doing but by developing a new goal that makes current performance appear to be less than "good enough." In a sense, a crisis is created when a CEO says: "I know we are doing quite well, but our goal now is not to just do well but to aim for the moon. Can we achieve that?" Then they take the necessary time and effort to sell the challenge.

Based on my experience with various firms, I believe the "selling process" must take employees through at least three distinct stages of development (see Exhibit 4-7).

Stage 1: Communicate the goal. First, there must be communication and explanation of the organization's new objective. People cannot get excited about a goal unless they first understand what is to be achieved and why. There must come a point when everyone can say, "I know *what* we are trying to achieve and I understand *why* we are trying to achieve it."

Stage 2: Create belief in the goal through early victories. The second stage is more difficult. In this stage, company leaders need to convince employees that the objective is realistic and achievable. Employees should emerge from this stage thinking, "Yes, I think we can achieve this objective." This is more difficult than it sounds. While ambitious and stretching goals are needed to generate excitement, it is exactly these kinds of goals that tend to generate disbelief and dismissal as unrealistic and unachievable. To make these goals believable, you need to go beyond words.

One way to convince employees that the task before them is achievable is to create several early victories. Employees must be given proof that the ambitious goal is in fact within their reach. Thus, some early victories must follow soon after the announcement of the corporate objective, even if these victories are manufactured. The organization needs to create them, celebrate them, and use them to build momentum toward and enthusiasm for the corporate objective.

Stage 3: Solidify emotional commitment to the goal. Finally comes the most difficult stage of the selling process, when people have to move from rational acceptance of the objective to emotional commitment. This is a magical jump, and at the end of it people should be saying, "Yes, I know what the objective is, I understand why we are aiming for it, I believe we can achieve it, and I am personally committed to achieving it." This leap is extremely difficult to

Exhibit 4-7   Selling a Stretching Goal

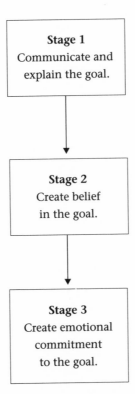

make, and you will likely need to employ a variety of tactics to pull it off. The development of emotional commitment is discussed in more detail in Chapter 5.

The experience of Douwe Egberts—a subsidiary of Sara Lee and the market leader in ground coffee and coffee systems in Europe— in "selling" its new "Vision 2005" challenge to employees high-lights the difficulties and frustrations of trying to sell an organiza-tional objective to hundreds of people. Despite being financially successful, the company decided to rejuvenate itself by developing a challenging new goal. The process was initiated in November 1995, when the top twenty managers from across the globe came together to analyze their environment and develop a new objective and a new strategy.

The new objective was communicated to the top 180 managers in a two-day conference in April 1996. During this conference, a variety of tactics were used to communicate the new objective and to explain why the company was embarking on such a journey. The managers were then asked to return to their country sub-sidiaries and inform all of their employees of the need to achieve this new goal. They were also asked to consider how the new objec-tive could be reflected in their annual operating plans. So as to gen-erate momentum, a few successful projects that were initiated after the November 1995 meeting were introduced at the conference (for example, the successful introduction of a new product in Spain was announced). These projects represented early victories in achieving the new objective.

This process was repeated at the company level every year over the period 1995–98. In addition, every country subsidiary orga-nized one-day events to communicate the new goal, explain why it was necessary, and galvanize employees to try to achieve it. Need-less to say, a huge amount of energy, resources, and time have been invested in the process to make sure that most people in the orga-nization are motivated to meet the new challenge. Three years into this plan, the CEO, Jacques A. N. Van Dijk, expressed the opinion that only then was the rest of the organization *beginning* to believe that "the new objective is here to stay." Three years of hard work and only then are people beginning to believe in this objective!

Who knows how long it would take to actually convince them to go for it.

To summarize: Another tactic that can be used to galvanize the organization into questioning the way it operates is to create a positive crisis by developing a new stretching objective. But this objective will be nothing but empty words unless the organization takes the time and makes the effort to sell it to employees and thereby gain their emotional commitment.

Build Slack into the System

A fourth means for the firm to stay flexible is to build a degree of slack into the system—even if this is inefficient in the short term. The logic behind such an approach is that since a firm cannot anticipate or predict everything, the best it can do is to develop the ability to react quickly to whatever the future might bring.

As mentioned above, if a firm is to react quickly to change, it must be willing to change and it must be capable of changing. Willingness to change results from a culture that welcomes change and an attitude that questions current practices and encourages experimentation with new ideas. As explained above, a firm can use a variety of tactics to develop such a questioning attitude and innovative culture.

On the other hand, being able to change when the need arises requires more than just willingness—the firm must have at its disposal the bundle of resources and capabilities that the new environment requires. The argument is that a firm should build a portfolio of diverse capabilities so that when the environment changes, it has the right competencies to compete effectively in the new environment. Several tactics can be used to build up capabilities: you can build them internally, as explained in the next chapter; you can acquire them through strategic alliances or outright acquisitions, as IBM does; you can buy equity-stake positions in new start-up firms, as Intel does; and so on. Unfortunately, as demanding as the task of building capabilities might be, it is not the most difficult aspect of developing the capability to respond to a changing environment. The real problem, given an uncertain future, lies in knowing which capabilities to develop.

Thus, advising companies to build their skills and competencies to prepare for the future simply begs the questions: "*Which* core competencies should we build? Which new ideas should we invest in?" The simple answer is: "You don't know." The problem with good ideas is that you can tell that they are good only after the fact. Lack of certainty, however, is no excuse for not trying. So you should be willing to experiment with new ideas and see if they work out. But what does that mean? Should a company place bets on anything and everything that moves?

To answer this question, consider why the capitalist system prevailed while the socialist system foundered.[15] The basic difference between the two is that in the socialist system, somebody tries to decide beforehand what is a good idea and then allocates resources accordingly. In the capitalist system, on the other hand, there is no central coordinating mechanism. Nobody tries to outsmart the market. Instead, multiple bets (that is, initiatives) are made, and through some selection process (which is not necessarily efficient in any sense) winners and losers emerge. The capitalist system is certainly "wasteful"—and it has been criticized as such—but it is the best engine of progress designed so far.

What characterizes successful strategic innovators is their ability to incorporate these essential features of the capitalist system into their organizations. By this, I mean that they have purposefully created internal variety by nurturing a variety of capabilities or experimenting with a variety of products and technologies (even at the expense of efficiency), and they have then allowed the outside market to decide which products and services are winners and which are losers. Thus, what you see in many strategic innovators is the harmonious coexistence of often conflicting features (variety) that are continually tested in the market and, if found wanting, are eliminated without too much debate.

Consider, for example, the case of Microsoft. As one observer noted in 1997:

> In the late 1980s, with DOS coming to the end of its useful life, Bill Gates focused on moving the industry to another Microsoft product, Windows. Appreciating the uncertainty of this punctuation point, however, he hedged his bet by also investing in Windows' competitors: Unix, OS/2, and the Apple Macintosh system. In addition, his company developed deep generic skills in object-oriented programming and

graphical interface design—skills that would be useful no matter which system won, even if it were a complete unknown. Gates's approach of pursuing several paths simultaneously is intrinsically difficult to manage. He was accused in the press of not having a strategy and confusing customers, and it is easy to imagine that there were internal tensions within Microsoft as well.[16]

Another good illustration of my point is provided by France's Leclerc. Leclerc was founded in the late 1950s by Eduard Leclerc, who gave up a career as a Catholic priest to start a supermarket dedicated to offering branded products at cheap prices. The organization has been very successful and has grown to a chain of more than 500 hypermarkets (that is, Wal-Mart–type stores that carry food, clothing, and many other kinds of products). It is now expanding into overseas markets.

Leclerc is a master at balancing quite a few conflicting forces: it has achieved low cost and differentiation simultaneously; it is very decentralized in some ways and yet centralized in others; it is a group of many small autonomous units yet still enjoys the benefits of size; it is structured as a federation of independent stores yet behaves as an integrated network; it encourages experimentation with new products and concepts yet survives the inevitable losses without pain; its employees feel and behave like "owners" of the organization yet own no stock; the whole organization behaves like one big family yet is a money-making machine. How could Leclerc have achieved such internal variety and how does it manage that variety?

The answer to this question is multifaceted. First, Leclerc is not a single company. Each store is owned and operated by individuals who choose to trade under the Leclerc name. But they are not franchisees, either: they do not have to pay for the right to trade under the Leclerc name. In fact, as described below, they receive numerous additional benefits from their Leclerc association for which they pay no charges. However, they agree to abide by certain norms and regulations—the primary one being that they will never be undersold by competitors. In addition, no individual—including members of the Leclerc family—may own more than two stores.

Each store has autonomy over its affairs. For example, given each store's unique geographic location—and therefore different type of customer—each store is free to decide what products to sell, what prices to charge, what promotions to run, and so on. In addition, each store can find its own suppliers and negotiate its own prices.

Such decentralization and autonomy encourages experimentation and achieves differentiation, but not at the expense of low cost. For example, each region has its own warehouse, which is owned by the member stores. The warehouse orders (and stores) on behalf of all its members those types of products that do not need to be sold fresh, thereby achieving purchasing economies. In addition, a central purchasing department in Paris identifies potential suppliers and negotiates prices with them. Individual stores are not obligated to work with any supplier recommended by the center, but this method certainly allows purchasing economies. The use of the Leclerc name by all also achieves advertising and promotional benefits and cuts costs. Finally, new Leclerc stores are always started by current Leclerc employees who receive the financial backing and guarantees of current Leclerc store owners. The financial backing of a prominent local businessperson is beneficial in securing start-up capital from banks.

In addition, every store owner is active in the management of the whole organization. The owners attend monthly regional meetings, as well as frequent national meetings, where they make decisions and exchange experiences. Stores belong to regions, and each region is "run" by a member for three years (on a voluntary basis of course). Not only does the region president run the affairs of the region, but he or she travels extensively to individual stores to offer advice, monitor plans, and share best practices. Furthermore, at the end of every year, each store owner has to distribute 25 percent of the store's profits to its employees. Store owners also have the "duty" (not obligation) to act as "godparents" to one of their employees. The selected employee is someone with high potential to become a Leclerc store owner. This person receives continual support and advice and, if and when the time comes, financial backing and moral support to start a store. If the new store fails, the "godparent" is financially liable for any liabilities.

How is so much variety managed? Information systems are used to monitor what is happening across the "federation." Frequent meetings also help to foster the exchange of ideas and monitor progress. However, the two primary mechanisms of control are (1) a common and deeply felt vision that sets the parameters within which each member store operates and (2) a strong family culture in which everyone is treated with fairness and openness. Each store has its own unique culture (created primarily by the personality of the store owner). Yet a "common" Leclerc culture permeates the organization, setting the parameters, the accepted norms, the shared values, and the constraints within which individuals behave. It is this shared culture that provides for so much autonomy and freedom without the accompanying fear that somebody, somewhere, will do something nasty.

There are still more elements of the Leclerc organization worth mentioning. However, what I have already described should illustrate vividly what I mean when I suggest that successful strategic innovators create the necessary internal variety and then let the market decide what wins and what loses. At any given time, one thousand experiments are taking place within Leclerc, all of them conducted within accepted parameters and on the initiative of an individual. Nobody knows which of these experiments will succeed and which will fail. But out of this experimentation, winners do emerge—that is, practices and products that the consumers themselves chose as winners. These "winners" are quickly picked up by the rest of the organization and become part of day-to-day business. The losers, on the other hand, die a quick death.[17]

Summary

1. In deciding how to play the game, a firm must not only identify what activities it needs to perform but also combine these activities into a reinforcing system that creates the requisite fit between what the environment needs and what the company does.

2. At the same time, the company must never forget that the environment outside the firm is in a constant state of flux. This does not mean that the firm must not strive to achieve fit! It must create this fit, but it must also remain flexible enough to respond to the ever-changing environment. Hence, the firm must aim to achieve *dynamic* fit with its environment.

3. A firm can use a variety of tactics to achieve dynamic fit with its environment. For example, it may:

- build internal variety that will allow it to develop competencies even before it even knows which competencies will be needed.

- institutionalize continual innovation.

- develop a culture that welcomes change—accomplishing this by creating uneven, episodic crises rather than actions aimed at continuous improvement.

- develop a strategic monitoring system that warns of inflexion points in its future well in advance.

- prevent core competencies from becoming core rigidities.

5

Identify and Secure
Strategic Assets and Capabilities

Core competencies are the wellspring of new business development.
They should constitute the focus for strategy at the corporate level.

—C. K. Prahalad and Gary Hamel, "The Core Competence of the
Corporation"

The spirit of Southwest is the most difficult thing to emulate. If we
ever do lose that, we will have lost our most valuable competitive
asset.

—Herb Kelleher, CEO, Southwest Airlines

In Chapter 4, I argued that strategy is all about combining activities into a reinforcing system that creates a dynamic fit with the environment. But to carry out these activities, a firm needs to access and utilize a complex set of tangible and intangible assets, skills, and capabilities. For example, to reap the benefits of scale economies in production, the firm will require tangible assets, such as a large-scale plant, and intangible assets, such as the skills to manage this facility effectively and distributor loyalty to support a constant high volume of sales. Therefore, after deciding what activities the company will perform (that is, after deciding on the "how" question), the company needs to consider the question, "What assets, skills, and capabilities should we now build to enable us to carry out these activities?"

Of course, a firm's current stock of assets and capabilities will influence what activities the firm chooses to perform. Therefore, the thinking process involved in deciding these issues is not (and should not) be linear. In other words, a firm can start out by asking,

"What activities should I perform in this market?" And, after deciding on the activities, tackle the issue of what skills and capabilities to develop. Alternatively, the firm can first ask the question, "What skills and capabilities do I currently have?" After answering this question, it can tackle the question "Given my current stock of capabilities, what activities should I perform in the market?"

There have been many arguments and debates in the business literature as to the correct sequence of these questions. Do you build your strategy on an assessment of what skills and capabilities you have, or do you first decide on a strategy (based on some kind of industry analysis) and then decide on what skills and capabilities to build? As I argue in Chapter 7, it's not an either/or issue: both approaches must be utilized, and innovation will take place if the mind is forced to think about these issues from as many different angles as possible. Whatever approach is utilized, understanding what assets and capabilities the firm will need and how to build them is an important element of any strategy. Not all assets and capabilities are equally valuable, however. To be effective, strategy must therefore focus on building not just any capability that might be needed but the capabilities that are truly valuable.

What Makes an Asset or Capability Truly Valuable

A firm can secure assets and capabilities in four basic ways.[1] It may obtain them with the *endowment* that established the business. For example, a company established to exploit a proprietary technology may have received a valuable patent from its founder. It may *acquire* the assets on the open market or contract directly for the services of an asset (as in the case of an equipment lease). It may access the required asset or capability by *sharing* it with a subsidiary or an alliance partner. Finally, it can *accumulate* the required asset through learning by doing over time.

The skills, resources, assets, and competencies that are truly valuable to the firm are those which cannot be imitated by others in a competitive market (through one of the four mechanisms identified above) or substituted by some other asset that can be purchased competitively. Researchers exploring the implications of the resource-based view of the firm have used the term *strategic assets* to denote the skills, resources, assets, and competencies that are valuable in this sense.[2] Following are the characteristics that define a strategic asset:

It is rare. Even if the capability or resource you possess is valuable, if everybody else has it, it will not provide you (or anyone else) with a competitive advantage. Therefore, for an asset to be valuable, it has to be rare—that is, not available to your competitors. For example, in the period 1966–76, the British company Laker Airways became very successful in the packaged holiday business on the basis of a low-cost infrastructure. Using its low-cost advantages, Laker then attacked British Airways and other U.S.-based major airlines in the mid-1970s. This effort failed, and the airline went bankrupt in 1982. The reason? British Airways used its reservations systems and skills in yield management to offer comparably low prices. The skills and competencies that Laker was transferring to the trans-Atlantic airline business—though valuable—were not rare enough to provide the company with a sustainable advantage.

As another example of the same principle, consider Caterpillar, a giant in the manufacture of earth-moving equipment.[3] Caterpillar's success is based on an excellent service and supply network. This competence allows it to transport and service heavy construction equipment all over the world at very low cost. How did Caterpillar develop this competence? Through the government support it received during World War II, when it became the exclusive supplier to the Department of War (now the Department of Defense). Because another company would have to receive similar government support to develop such a competence quickly and cost-effectively (which is unlikely), this competence is rare and represents a source of advantage for Caterpillar.

It is not easy to imitate. Even if your competitors do not currently have the valuable asset you possess (that is, it is rare), if it costs them very little to replicate it, they soon will, and your advantage will be gone. For example, one of Wal-Mart's core competencies has been its point-of-purchase data-collection skill, which allows Wal-Mart to control its inventory efficiently and respond to changes in consumer tastes quickly and flexibly. This competence gave Wal-Mart an advantage over competitors such as Kmart during the 1980s. However, this advantage has now been effectively neutralized because Kmart has imitated this competence.[4] On the other hand, 3M continues to diversify profitably by capitalizing on a competence that is extremely difficult for competitors to imitate: its innovative culture and entrepreneurial organization. Although nearly every organization pays lip service to innovation and creativity, very few companies achieve these difficult-to-imitate competencies.

It is not easy to substitute. An asset will lose its strategic value not only if it can be easily duplicated by competitors but also if another asset can easily substitute for it. For example, Canon substituted distribution dealers for one of Xerox's strong competencies in the copier business—its superb sales force. Dell substituted direct-to-customer sales for IBM's dealers and sales force. First Direct substituted telephone banking for Barclays' extensive branch network in the U.K. banking industry. On the other hand, try as they might, Pepsi and other soft drink competitors cannot replicate or find a substitute for Coca-Cola's strong brand name. That asset gives Coke a lasting advantage.

To assess whether the assets you are trying to exploit are indeed strategic, you should be asking these kinds of questions: How many of my competitors already possess this asset? Do firms without this asset face a cost disadvantage in obtaining it? Is it possible to substitute another asset for this one? It is the utilization of *strategic* assets and capabilities, not just any asset or capability, that leads to success in the market. To identify opportunities for profitable growth, companies need to first identify such strategic assets and then develop their activities around them, using the strategic assets as building blocks.

How to Accumulate Strategic Assets and Capabilities

Firms that are able to accumulate strategic assets and capabilities more quickly or at less cost than their competitors will be at a competitive advantage. A firm can do so in a number of ways.

One way to accumulate strategic assets is through continual learning.[5] A firm should be capable not only of learning but also of consciously using this learning to reduce costs and increase the speed at which it can accumulate new strategic assets. It is therefore crucial for firms to develop structures and processes that facilitate and promote learning across different functions and divisions. Such internal mechanisms include the transfer of key people across functions, the use of business integrators whose job it is to move around the organization and spread best practices, the creation of champions in each area of competence, the use of company newsletters or regular conferences to communicate best practices, the organization of competence communities, and the development of a learning culture.[6] In addition, as I explain in the next chapter, for learning to take place, the firm must create an "organizational environment" that promotes this kind of behavior.

Another way to accumulate strategic assets is to use the firm's competencies to build new assets more quickly or more cheaply than competitors do. Consider, for example, how Canon outcompeted Xerox in the copier business. When Canon diversified from cameras to copiers, its camera division had already developed a series of competencies, including knowledge of how to increase the effectiveness of a dealer network, how to develop new products combining optics and electronics, and how to squeeze more productivity out of high-volume assembly lines. All this knowledge is directly applicable to the copier business. As a result, Canon could use its accumulated knowledge in the camera business to improve the quality of its processes in the copier business and so compete with Xerox on an equal or even superior footing, despite Xerox's longer experience in copiers.

A third way to develop new strategic assets and capabilities is through the use of a *strategic staircase*.[7] This is a tool that allows companies to first identify what capabilities they will need to achieve their strategic objective and then to break this "capabilities gap" down into smaller pieces that employees can focus on. Here I'll use Canon's strategy for entering the copier business to demonstrate how the strategic staircase can work.

As shown in Exhibit 5-1 (which flows from right to left), Canon decided in the early 1960s to diversify from cameras into

Exhibit 5-1 Canon's Strategic Staircase

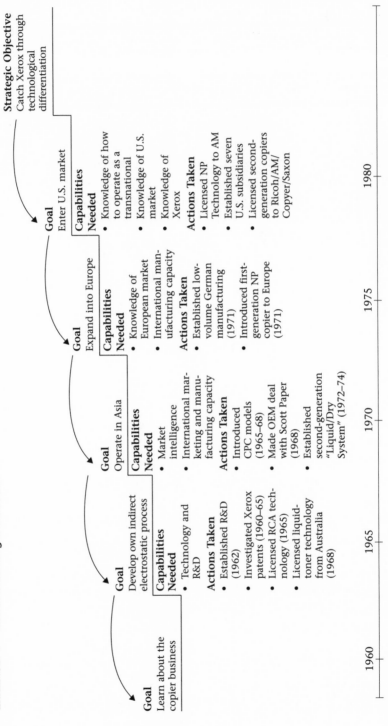

Strategic Objective
Catch Xerox through technological differentiation

Goal
Enter U.S. market

Capabilities Needed
- Knowledge of how to operate as a transnational
- Knowledge of U.S. market
- Knowledge of Xerox

Actions Taken
- Licensed NP Technology to AM
- Established seven U.S. subsidiaries
- Licensed second-generation copiers to Ricoh/AM/ Copyer/Saxon

Goal
Expand into Europe

Capabilities Needed
- Knowledge of European market
- International manufacturing capacity

Actions Taken
- Established low-volume German manufacturing (1971)
- Introduced first-generation NP copier to Europe (1971)

Goal
Operate in Asia

Capabilities Needed
- Market intelligence
- International marketing and manufacturing capacity

Actions Taken
- Introduced CPC models (1965–68)
- Made OEM deal with Scott Paper (1968)
- Established second-generation "Liquid/Dry System" (1972–74)

Goal
Develop own indirect electrostatic process

Capabilities Needed
- Technology and R&D

Actions Taken
- Established R&D (1962)
- Investigated Xerox patents (1960–65)
- Licensed RCA technology (1965)
- Licensed liquid-toner technology from Australia (1968)

Goal
Learn about the copier business

1960   1965   1970   1975   1980

photocopiers, attacking Xerox in the process. From the beginning, Canon set as its strategic ambition the objective of "catching" Xerox through technological differentiation. The development of such a stretching long-term goal is the first step in building a strategic staircase.

Working backward from the long-term objective, Canon developed a series of intermediate goals. The thinking went as follows: If the company was to achieve its long-term goal by 1980, where did it need to be in 1975? The answer was that it needed to be operating in Europe, a goal that became a milestone. In turn, if it was to be fully operational in Europe by 1975, where should it be in 1970? Operating all over Asia by 1970, which became another milestone. Similarly, for the 1970 goal to be achieved, the milestone of developing its own technology by 1965 had to be set.

Note that this process of goal setting is the opposite of the norm. Most companies start from the present and establish objectives for the next year or for the next five or ten years. The process I am proposing starts from the end and works back to the start date. In addition, each goal is not a mere projection of the present—it is a clear step that will advance the firm's progress toward the long-term objective.

Having developed a staircase of goals, Canon could then *look forward* and think about the sequence in which it would have to develop new skills and capabilities. Starting from the early 1960s, it realized that if it were to achieve its 1965 goal, it needed to invest heavily in research and development. Thus, learning about the technology and overcoming Xerox's patents became the first capability to build. Looking further ahead, Canon realized that if it were to achieve its 1970 goal, it had to learn about international marketing. So it established a joint venture agreement with Scott Paper to develop this capability. Looking even further out, Canon realized that to achieve its 1975 goal, it needed to acquire international manufacturing expertise. And it did so.

Notice that this process forces the company to focus on required skills and capabilities in a sequential manner. Dividing the ultimate requirement into a series of smaller steps to close a capabilities gap makes the overall task less daunting and allows for the achievement of early victories that can generate enthusiasm. The sequence is also important, because employees can see that each step is not isolated but is part of a staircase to the promised land.

Of course, there is a logic to the sequence: we need to achieve X before we move to Y, which means we need to develop capability A before B. This inevitably requires that explicit and clearly communicated choices be made and adhered to, such as, "This year we will invest in capability A but *not* B." Saying no to one thing in favor of another is difficult. Often, companies want to have their cake and eat it, a desire that leads to unfocused efforts in which people try to do a little bit of this and a little bit of that. Strong leadership is required to make these difficult tradeoffs.

Consider, for example, what Jan Carlzon, the CEO who turned around Scandinavian carrier SAS in the early 1980s, had to say:

> You must provide a framework in which people can act. For example, we have said that our first priority is safety, second is punctuality, and third is other services. So, if you risk flight safety by leaving on time, you have acted outside the framework of your authority. The same is true if you don't leave on time because you are missing two catering boxes of meat. That's what I mean by a framework. You give people a framework, and within this framework you let people act . . . the dangerous thing is to not make decisions.[8]

In summary, developing a strategic staircase involves three steps:

1. Develop the firm's overall strategic objective.

2. Working *backward* from this long-term objective, develop the medium- and short-term goals that need to be achieved if the long-term goal is to be achieved.

3. Working *forward* from the present, identify the sequence of skills and capabilities needed to achieve each successive goal on the staircase, and then invest to develop those skills.

Michael Hay and Peter Williamson, who developed the strategic staircase as a managerial tool, have proposed five principles to maximize its effectiveness:

1. The strategic objective must be defined clearly, concisely, and in terms that are motivating.

2. Skills and capabilities must be developed in a deliberate and sequential manner. The precise order in which capabilities will be developed must be specified and explained to employees.

3. Difficult choices on what to invest in and what not to invest in must be made.

4. Timetables must be agreed on for the building of the different steps in the staircase.

5. Measures by which progress on the initiatives will be judged must be defined and used.[9]

While building the skills and capabilities that will allow it to achieve its strategic objective, a company must also prepare itself for changes in its environment that might require a change of direction and a different set of needed capabilities. As I argued in Chapter 4, the difficulty for any company lies in the fact that it cannot predict with 100 percent accuracy how the future may unfold, hence, it cannot know for sure what capabilities it should build.

The solution to this predicament lies in developing a diverse portfolio of capabilities so as to increase the probability that the firm will have those it needs no matter how the future unfolds. Note, however, that while this solution increases the probability that the firm will get lucky, it does not eliminate all the risk. No matter how many capabilities you develop, you still run the risk of running into a future that is so radically different from what you expected that you couldn't possibly prepare for it. Nor does the development of a diverse set of capabilities mean that top management should not take a position on how it expects the future to unfold. To see this point, consider Exhibit 5-2.

For a company at the center point, the future might unfold in any of the directions shown by the arrows. If the future unfolds in the northeasterly direction, then capabilities A and B will be needed. On the other hand, if the future unfolds in the southwesterly direction, capabilities G and H will be needed. And so on. The firm cannot possibly invest in everything. It must therefore choose.

How do you choose? Top managers must make their best estimate as to how the future will unfold and base their investment decisions on this vision of the future. This vision does not have to

Exhibit 5-2 Staking Out Future Territory

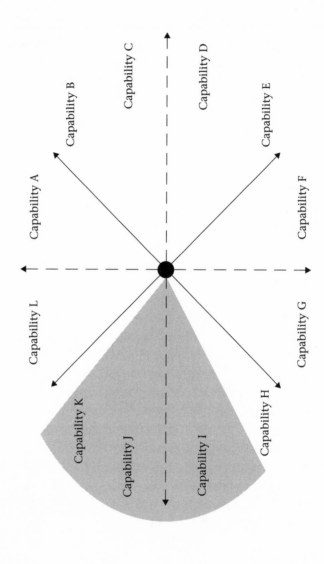

be an exact point in the future—it can be a range, as shown by the shaded region in the exhibit. In effect, management is saying: "I don't know for sure how the future will unfold but I am confident it will be in the shaded region." This implies that the company will invest in building capabilities I, J and K. If the future actually unfolds as predicted, then the firm survives and prospers. If it doesn't, then chances are the company dies. The risk of making the wrong call is real, but it cannot be used as an excuse for not making choices.

How to Win Emotional Commitment to the Strategy

Any strategy, if it is to succeed, needs the emotional commitment of the people who are to advance it. As explained briefly in Chapter 4, emotional commitment is different from rational commitment. The latter simply means that people have agreed at an intellectual level to the good sense of what you are proposing. It does not mean that they are prepared to *do* anything about it. Nor does it mean that they will change their behavior to support the objectives they have agreed to. But if you succeed in winning people's emotional commitment, they will not only do what you are proposing but they will do it passionately and enthusiastically. The physical signs that emotional commitment from employees has been achieved are passion, excitement, energy, and pride. For such a dramatic change of attitude to occur, people must not only accept and agree with the strategy—they must buy into it. How, then, do you win them over?

Winning people's emotional commitment is a four-stage process, as shown in Exhibit 5-3. The process proposed here is very similar to that outlined in Chapter 4 for selling a stretching objective to employees. As is to be expected, the process takes time, but it is well worth the effort. Without emotional commitment, even the most brilliant strategies will fail.

In stage 1, your goal is to clearly explain the strategy. People will not be receptive to the plan unless they understand what it is and why it is worth doing. At this early stage, you do not necessarily expect people to agree with the strategy. If you get agreement, fine.

But if you don't, it is not fatal. You simply need to explain the strategy and the reasons why it has been adopted. The communication stage will go more smoothly if people have been involved in developing the strategy or if the strategy is simple and explicit. At the end of this stage, people should be saying: "I know and understand what our strategy is."

In stage 2, your goal is to secure people's agreement to pursue the strategy. Again, people are more likely to agree with it if they were consulted on or involved in its development. Similarly, the strategy is more likely to win acceptance if you spend time and effort explaining it. Reasoned argument, open debate, and an environment that allows for criticism and disagreement all help in winning people over. The use of "allies" to argue your case on your behalf can also help, as can the use of examples and facts, such as

Exhibit 5-3 Winning Emotional Commitment to Strategy

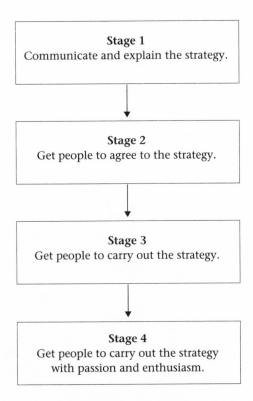

Stage 1
Communicate and explain the strategy.

Stage 2
Get people to agree to the strategy.

Stage 3
Get people to carry out the strategy.

Stage 4
Get people to carry out the strategy
with passion and enthusiasm.

trends in the market, actions by competitors, changing demo-graphics, and the like. The object of this stage is for people to say: "I agree with our chosen strategy."

So far, all that has been achieved is rational commitment, which does not necessarily translate into action. To persuade people not only to agree to the strategy but to enact it is the objective of stage 3. Remember: just because people agree to do something does not mean they will do it.

Why is it that people often do not do what they've agreed to do? Perhaps their "agreement" is less than genuine, made for political or other reasons. Or perhaps they want to act but they cannot—either they are not empowered to act or the organization's environment precludes action. This is a crucial point: *Environment creates behavior.* If you want people to act on a strategy, you must first establish the appropriate environment for them to do so. I return to this point in the next chapter.

The way people assign priorities may also account for their lack of follow-through. As busy people with too many things to do at any one time, we may simply never get to our low-priority tasks, even if we have agreed to do them. What is required to implement the strategy, then, is to find ways to change people's priorities. The firm may, for example, institute changes in evaluation and reward procedures. As the saying goes: "What gets measured, gets done."

It may also be necessary to make individuals responsible for specific tasks. Too often, people hide behind the word "we"—as in "We did not do this because. . . ." Making individuals responsible for specific tasks for which they will be evaluated and rewarded is a powerful means of ensuring that these tasks move up on your people's priority lists.

In the fourth and final stage of winning commitment to your strategy, you go for the gold—that is, emotional commitment. The end-result should be passionate and single-minded pursuit of our strategy by everyone in the organization. Such commitment will *slowly* emerge when a company builds momentum through early victories and success; when leaders in the organization demonstrate through word and deed that they are personally committed to the strategy; when the organization creates a supportive atmosphere that allows people to take the initiative and contribute to the achievement of the strategy; when people see some tangible benefit to be gained by implementing the strategy; and when the initial implementation of the strategy leads to quick successes. Without doubt, winning emotional commitment to a strategy requires time, effort, and commitment from top management. It is hard to achieve, but without it, the strategy—however good in theory—will not succeed in practice.

One of the best-known examples in which emotional commitment to a strategy was won in an impressive manner is that of Apple Computers in the mid-1980s. After its initial success in 1976–81, Apple came under severe attack from IBM, which entered the market in 1981 with its own computer, the IBM PC. At that time, industry analysts predicted that Apple would lose the battle and be forced out of business.

Apple's CEO, Steve Jobs, responded to the threat by setting up a separate team to develop a new computer, the Macintosh. The team was separated from the rest of the Apple organization and was given freedom and resources to innovate. Team members were very carefully recruited, and only those who demonstrated passionate belief in developing a product that would change the way people thought about computers were allowed to join the team. Team members were made to feel that they were on a grand mission to change the world and save everybody from "evil" IBM. This sense of self-importance was reinforced by selective recruitment, by the challenge embodied in the team's objective, by the presence of a big and threatening enemy (IBM), and by the fact that Steve Jobs himself (that is, the leader) spent most of his time working with this team rather than with the rest of Apple.

Not only was the team placed in a separate building but it was also given freedom and autonomy to experiment and try things out. The group was encouraged to behave like a band of pirates outside the corporate bureaucracy. There was limited hierarchy in the team, and decisions were made after debates in a collective manner. The feeling was "We are in this together." In addition, people were allowed to dress as they liked and work the hours that suited them. To reinforce this sense of being "mavericks," a pirate's flag was placed on top of the building. Once the Mac was developed, the names of all team members were written on the inside of every computer—a gesture symbolizing the idea that this was the work of everyone on the team.

The Macintosh was released in 1984 and was a great success. It rejuvenated Apple and put the company back in the running with IBM. Even though this example describes what happened with a small group of people, the generic tactics used by Steve Jobs to win the group's emotional support do apply to larger groups and even entire companies (see Exhibit 5-4). Granted, it is easier to win over 50 people than 5,000, but the tactics that can be used are exactly the same. It just requires more effort and time.

All of these tactics are important and reinforce each other. However, by far the most effective is to make your employees feel proud

Exhibit 5-4   Apple Computers:
Tactics for Winning Emotional Commitment to Strategy

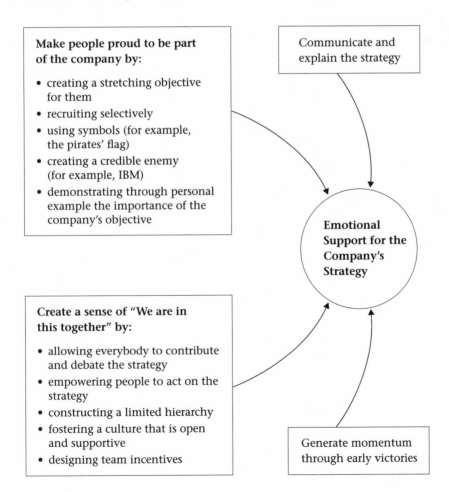

to be part of the company and proud for what it stands for or is trying to achieve. Once you achieve this, passion and emotional support for the company's strategy follow naturally.

Summary

1. Everything a firm does in its business must be supported by the necessary skills, resources, and capabilities. Thus, to carry out the activities that its strategy requires, a firm must first develop the necessary assets and capabilities.

2. The assets or capabilities that can provide the firm with sustainable advantage are those which are difficult for competitors to achieve: they are rare, they cannot be imitated, there is no real substitute for them. A firm must pay particular attention to developing these kinds of strategic capabilities.

3. New capabilities can be developed in a number of ways. One way is to build a strategic staircase, which can help companies identify and develop the capabilities they will need to achieve their long-term objectives in a sequential manner.

4. A strategy must have the emotional commitment of the people who will work toward its implementation. Merely asking for such commitment is not enough. To obtain real commitment, you must get people not only to accept and agree with the strategy but to buy into it.

6

Create the Right
Organizational Environment

The behavioral context of a company provide[s] people with a source of stimulation. Unfortunately, over time, many large companies have created a context more akin to the polluted, oppressive environment of the inner city in mid-summer, sapping personal energy and creating conditions for apathy.

—Christopher Bartlett and Sumantra Ghoshal, "Rebuilding Behavioral Context"

If literally thousands of players, from enormously diverse backgrounds, all generate the same qualitative behavior patterns, the causes of the behavior must lie beyond the individuals. The causes of the behavior must lie in the structure of the game itself.

—Peter Senge, *The Fifth Discipline*

In early 1996, the CEO of a major food multinational complained to his assembled senior management team that despite the obvious importance of, and his repeated calls for, closer cooperation between the national subsidiaries, they seemed to be drifting even further apart. To illustrate his point, he recalled how the Italian subsidiary had recently turned down a request from headquarters to transfer three top engineers from their posts in Italy to the German subsidiary. Even though the company stood to benefit from this transfer, the Italian subsidiary had refused to OK the transfer, arguing that the engineers were needed in Italy.

This experience reminded me of a complaint I had heard just a few months earlier, at the end of 1995, from a transport and logistics multinational based in the United Kingdom. The CEO and other top managers had discovered, much to their horror, that divisions were targeting customers that were delivering margins below the company's minimum threshold of 5 percent. They were quite surprised to learn this because they thought they had made it very clear that no one was to accept any customer that did not deliver a margin of at least 5 percent.

What's going on here? Why are the behaviors observed in these organizations so different from what their managers expected, namely, closer global integration in the case of the first company and targeting of profitable customers in the second? In both cases, the organization's desired strategic behavior was clearly communicated to all employees—yet they did not comply. What is the source of this mystery?

These two examples are not unique—in fact, they are the norm! In almost every company around the world this phenomenon repeats itself: the company adopts a certain strategy, yet people in the company behave in ways that do not support (or may even undermine) the strategy. Naturally, this divergence between desired and actual behavior is a source of frustration for top management. The usual response is to criticize employees and demand that they adopt the desired behavior. Unfortunately, this is wasted effort.

What top management forgets is that the single most important determinant of employee behavior is the underlying context or environment of the organization. It doesn't matter how many times you tell employees to do something or how often you stress the importance of behaving in a certain way. People will not comply until an organizational environment that promotes and supports the desired behavior has been created. Thus, if you want people to be more innovative, you must *first* create an underlying environment that promotes innovation. Similarly, if you want them to be more customer-oriented, you need to create an environment that encourages such behavior.

In the case of the first company mentioned above, the food multinational, its organizational structure and incentives were designed in a way that supported a local rather than global approach. For example, national subsidiaries were evaluated and rewarded on the basis of how well they did in their domestic markets; what incentive, then, did the Italian subsidiary have to give its best engineers to Germany? Similarly, the division managers of the logistics company were evaluated according to revenue growth; is it a surprise, then, that they chased down every customer in sight, even if these customers were not that profitable? In each case, the local managers were behaving rationally. Their behavior may not have been what top management desired, but, given their organizational environments, it was inevitable that these would be the behaviors to emerge.

The idea that a company's underlying environment conditions employee behavior is not new.[1] However, it has far-reaching implications for strategy. What it implies is that to develop a superior strategy, a company must not only decide on who, what, and how; it must also create an underlying environment that supports and promotes behaviors that reinforce the company's strategic decisions.[2] A company that wants its strategy to be implemented properly must ask and answer the question: "What organizational environment must I create internally to elicit the employee behavior that will support my chosen strategy?"

The Beer Game, or How Environment Creates Behavior

Over the past few years, executives throughout the world have been exposed to a fascinating "game" developed by Professors Jay Forrester and John Sterman at MIT. Originally known as the production-distribution game, it has been dubbed the beer game. One lesson of the beer game that comes over loud and clear to participants is that behavior is conditioned by environment. Therefore, to improve or change behaviors that we don't like, we must first change the underlying environment.

The game is played on a board that represents the production and distribution of beer.[3] Each board consists of a team of four players: retailer, wholesaler, distributor, and factory. Each simulated week, customers place an order with the retailer, who ships the requested beer (represented by pennies) out of his or her inventory and then places an order with the wholesaler. The wholesaler ships the beer requested by the retailer, then places an order with the distributor. Likewise, the distributor ships the order placed by the wholesaler and then places an order with the factory. The factory ships the order placed by the distributor and then manufactures more beer from its raw materials. At each of these stages, there are ordering and shipping delays. The players place their orders by writing them on pieces of paper, which they in turn pass on to their respective suppliers. Apart from these order slips, no communication among players is allowed.

The game is intended to be played for 50 weeks. The players' objective is to minimize *total* team costs. There are two types of cost in the game: inventory costs $0.50 per bottle of beer per week, while an order backlog (that is, inability to deliver) costs $1.00 per bottle. Thus, the players have to balance two opposing forces: they need to order enough beer so that they can supply from inventory whatever is ordered, but they must also be careful not to order too much, such that they accumulate expensive unused inventory.

I have now played this game with hundreds of executives from at least twenty-five different countries, ranging in age from twenty-five to fifty and in seniority from young managers to board directors. *No matter who plays the game, the patterns of behavior are the same each time.* For example, we always get people behaving in a very inefficient way. In fact, players behave so suboptimally that their team cost at the end of the game can amount to anything between $2,000 and $10,000. Very seldom does a team achieve a cost of less than $1,000. To put these results in perspective, the optimal performance for the game is a team cost well below $500. Thus, actual performance ranges from four to twenty times worse than optimal!

In addition to suboptimal performance, we get other common behavioral patterns every time we play the game. For example, fluctuations in the system always occur: orders and inventories rise and fall in waves. And the fluctuations become amplified as players progress from retailer to factory: the ups and downs in the orders placed increase steadily along the supply chain from customer to factory. For example, if the retailer increases his or her order by two beers, by the time the shock is transmitted down the line, the factory is increasing his or her order by up to twenty beers. This is usually blamed on lack of communication among the players, but, as I explain below, there is more to it than that.

To realize how surprising these fluctuations in the orders placed are, all you need to know is that end-customer demand (that is, the demand faced by the retailer) is actually kept constant through most of the game! It starts at four beers a week, rises to eight in the fifth week, and remains constant thereafter. When we reveal this in class, disbelief and despair follow. How is it possible, in a situation so (artificially) simple, that people's behavior falls so short of optimum?

It is easy to get people to realize and accept that their behavior has been suboptimal. After all, their costs are usually so high that there is no avoiding the fact! Real learning takes place when people attempt to understand *why* they behaved so inefficiently. A common first response is to blame other team members for overreacting or to blame game leaders for preventing players from communicating with each other. Although these are plausible reasons, the question is: "Why is it that no matter who is playing the game, the result is always suboptimal performance, characterized by fluctuations, amplifications, and phase lags?"

It soon becomes apparent that certain structural features of the game "force" every player into a certain predictable type of behavior. For example, the delays in the system (in ordering and delivering beer) induce people to overreact, or even panic, since it takes time for any inventory or backlog problems to be corrected. Similarly, the multiple layers in the system from retailer to factory amplify disturbances (such as an increase in orders at the retailer end) and create shock waves down the system. The situation is exacerbated by the lack of communication among players: because they have no information about what other players are doing or the pressures they are under, they forget all about *team* costs and try to optimize their little piece of the system. Unfortunately, failing to account for the impact of decisions and actions on teammates is disastrous because of the many interrelationships throughout the system.

This kind of thinking leads players to appreciate the most profound lesson of the beer game: how they behave in the game is almost outside their control. Their behavior is pretty much determined by the underlying structure of the game—the time delays, the lack of information, the inability to forecast, the multiple layers in the system. As Peter Senge argues in his book *The Fifth Discipline*, players become "prisoners" of the system: "When placed in the same system, people, however different, tend to produce similar results."[4]

The idea that the underlying structure of a system creates the behavior in that system is the first principle of the discipline of systems dynamics. As shown in Exhibit 6-1, this principle has immediate applicability in real-life work situations: the behavior we observe in companies is created by their organizational environment. Since it is the daily behavior of employees that supports or undermines a strategy, a company cannot implement its strategy properly unless it first creates an environment that produces the appropriate behavior in its employees.

The logical corollary to this is that if we change the environment, behavior will change as well. Recent research has demonstrated that this is exactly what happens.[5] The first graph in Exhibit 6-2 shows how players order beer over time in a typical beer game.

Exhibit 6-1   Structure Creates Behavior

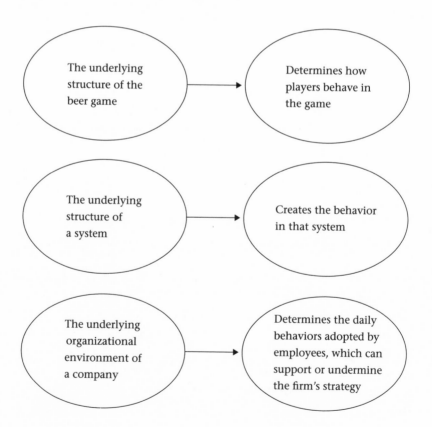

Exhibit 6-2 Improving Behavior in the Beer Game

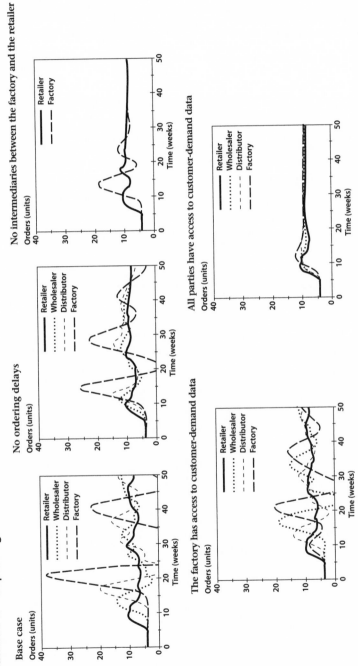

Source: Reprinted from *European Management Journal* 11, no. 4, Ann Van Ackere, Erik Reimer Larsen, and John D. W. Morecroft, "Systems Thinking and Business Process Redesign: An Application to the Beer Game," pp. 412–413. Copyright 1993, with permission from Elsevier Science.

The fluctuations in orders are obvious. The other four graphs show ordering behavior when (1) we remove ordering delays, (2) the wholesaler and distributor (the intermediaries) are removed from the supply chain, (3) the factory is given access to customer demand data, and (4) all players are given access to customer demand data.

The improvement in behavior is impressive. Note how the ups and downs in orders are not as pronounced as in the base case and almost disappear in the last graph. Note also how amplifications in the system (as we move from retailer to factory) are not as severe as in the base case. These are all indications that players behave much more efficiently as the underlying structure of the game is improved. As if by magic, "inefficient" people on the verge of being fired are transformed into superefficient managers who deserve to be promoted.

This result also has immediate applicability in real-life work situations: if for whatever reason we do not consider the behavior we observe in our company to be optimal, the first thing we must do is to "fix" the company's underlying environment. Desired behaviors, such as being innovative, trusting, customer-oriented, and the like, do not occur simply because you want them to occur; you must create an organizational environment from which they can emerge.[6]

What Is "Organizational Environment"?

When I use the term *organizational environment,*[7] I am referring to four basic elements:

1. The *culture* of the company, which includes its norms, values, and unquestioned assumptions.

2. The *structure* of the company, which comprises not only its formal hierarchy but also its physical setup and its systems (information, recruitment, market research, and so on).

3. The *incentives,* both monetary and nonmonetary, to perform well.

4. The *people,* including their skills and capabilities.

It is the combination of these four elements that creates the organizational environment, which in turn supports and promotes the firm's strategy (see Exhibit 6-3). Suppose, for example, that what you want to promote at your organization is the strategy of innovation. How might you achieve this?

To answer this question, consider the example of 3M, recognized as one of the world's most innovative companies. How has 3M maintained its high level of innovation, year after year? How does it support and promote its strategy of innovation? As suggested in Exhibit 6-4, which details the nature of the culture, structure, incentives, and people at 3M, the environment has been intentionally and explicitly designed to promote innovation.

At 3M, everyone is expected to take 15 percent of their time to work on unauthorized projects, as long as they are product-related. If an employee has a feasible idea, he or she can get a grant of up to $50,000 to pursue it. Top management continually encourages employees to experiment with new ideas. Employees are told that they are expected to innovate and will be evaluated accordingly. Every division is given the goal of achieving 25 percent of its sales in any given year from products introduced in the last five years. Implicit in all of this is the understanding that failure is acceptable, especially if it leads to new learning. This atmosphere is particularly appealing to people who are entrepreneurial by nature and willing to question the status quo. It also attracts to 3M some of the best scientists and engineers. (As does 3M's career path for scientists, which enables them to advance their careers without competing with business-type managers at the equivalent level in the company.)

Exhibit 6-3   The Organizational Environment Supporting Strategy

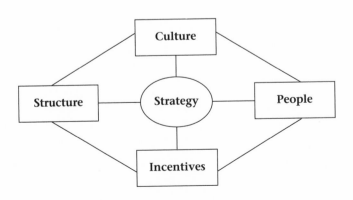

Exhibit 6-4 The Organizational Environment at 3M That Promotes Innovation

People

- By virtue of its incentives and culture, 3M attracts top scientists and engineers.
- The company is able to recruit and retain creative people with an entrepreneurial mindset.
- Because of its dual career ladder, top scientists can coexist with top managers without internal competition.

Culture

- 3M policy allows employees to spend 15 percent of their time developing projects of their own choosing.
- Employees are encouraged to take the initiative and are empowered to make decisions. Failure is accepted.
- The pervading culture is characterized by the rule that you have to kiss a lot of frogs to find one prince.
- A flat hierarchy makes people feel responsible for everything that goes on in their divisions.

Strategy

Incentives

- The company has established career ladders for scientists that are separate from those for managers.
- Teams that introduce successful new products are rewarded.
- Successful new products can be spun off as separate divisions with their own profit and loss statements. The original product champion becomes divisional president.
- 3M has set a formal goal that 25 percent of sales must come from new products. Managerial performance is measured and rewarded according to this goal.

Structure

- 3M utilizes cross-functional teams to work on research projects.
- Each team is headed by a "product champion" who is responsible for building team culture.
- One of 3M's top managers becomes a "management sponsor," who is to help the team secure resources and overcome bureaucratic obstacles.
- Divisions within 3M are run as separate companies. Divisional VPs have the same responsibility as a CEO in many other companies.
- Hierarchies within divisions are kept flat.
- The Annual Technology Fair allows scientists to showcase their latest research findings and exchange ideas and information.

To promote teamwork and multidisciplinary collaboration, 3M has established a system of cross-functional teams to work on new research projects. Each team is headed by a "product champion," who is responsible for developing the team culture. In addition, each team is "sponsored" by one of 3M's top managers, whose job it is to procure resources for the team and protect it from bureaucratic interference. To promote the transfer of ideas and best practices among scientists, 3M allows them to move freely from division to division to seek out projects throughout the company without formal approval. A companywide conference held every year at company expense allows scientists to present ideas to colleagues and seek advice.

Successful innovation is rewarded commensurably. Successful innovators receive not only public recognition for their work but also cash bonuses, salary increases, and promotions. If an innovation grows big enough, it is spun off as a separate division and the original product champion becomes division president. This is a powerful incentive to innovate.

All in all, 3M has designed its organizational environment—its culture, structure, incentives, and people—to support and promote the strategy of innovation. The fact that 3M has emerged as one of the most innovative companies in the world is not a matter of accident or luck but careful design.

A similar picture has emerged at Raychem, a corporation that supplies technology-intensive products to industrial customers in sectors such as aerospace, autos, and telecommunications. Like 3M, Raychem is a recognized innovator. When asked for the secret of innovation, Raychem's founder and CEO Paul Cook came up with the following elements:

- To be an innovative company, you have to ask for innovation. You assemble a group of talented people who are eager to do new things and put them in an environment where innovation is expected. It's that simple—and that hard.

- The most important thing we do is build an organization—a culture, if you'll pardon the word—that encourages teamwork, that encourages fun and excitement, that encourages everyone to do things differently and better—and that acknowledges and rewards people who excel.

- You also have to make sure your company has the brightest people in your core technologies. . . . You make sure those people talk to each other, that there is regular and intensive interchange between all those disciplines. They have to work together, communicate, sweat, swear, and do whatever it takes to extract from the core technology every product possibility.

- Size is the enemy of innovation. You can't get effective innovation in environments of more than a few hundred people. That's why as we continue to grow, we want Raychem to feel and function less like a giant corporation than a collection of small groups, each of which has its own technical people, marketing people, engineering people, manufacturing people.

- Innovation happens in pockets, and the location of those pockets changes over time. So, we want to play musical chairs with people and make extensive use of skunk works and project teams.

- The most important factor [that motivates people to focus on innovation] is individual recognition—more important than salaries, bonuses, or promotions. Most people, whether they are engineers, business managers, or machine operators, want to be creative. They want to identify with the success of their profession and their organization. They want to contribute to giving society more comfort, better health, more excitement. And their greatest reward is receiving acknowledgment that they did contribute to making something meaningful happen.[8]

Note that Cook's comments map to the four elements of organizational environment just described: culture, structure, incentives, and people. If innovation is to occur, these elements must promote and encourage it.

Here as with the other aspects of strategy I have discussed, the way the components of a system fit together is just as important as the components themselves.[9] In other words, the four elements that make up a firm's organizational environment must first fit and support each other and then combine to form a system that supports and promotes the firm's chosen strategy. Therefore, the challenge in constructing and promoting a strategy involves not only developing the four elements that constitute a firm's organizational environment but also putting them together in a self-reinforcing system.

Strategic failure usually occurs either when there is a poor fit between strategy and one or more components of the organizational environment or when the four components are in conflict with one another. For example, one common problem is the existence of a hierarchical and bureaucratic organizational structure alongside a strategy that calls for rapid new product development and continual improvement. Another common misfit is the existence of incentives that reward and encourage behavior that is inconsistent with the firm's espoused strategy. Yet another common type of misfit is a culture that focuses on the short term—on meeting next year's operating plan—while the strategy calls for long-term investments and the development of new technologies or products. All in all, without a good fit between a firm's strategy and its organizational environment, the whole edifice will collapse like a castle in the sand. Similarly, there is no situation more dysfunctional than that of entrepreneurial people working in a bureaucratic culture where everything must be done by the book, or of an incentive policy that emphasizes promotion in a flat hierarchy. Unless the four components that make up the firm's organizational environment fit with and support one another, the firm's strategy will be built on a faulty infrastructure.

Creating the appropriate fit between a firm's strategy and its organizational environment does not mean that the firm is sacrificing its flexibility. As I argued before, a firm must create the necessary fit while at the same time instilling the necessary flexibility in its systems and processes. I described how to achieve this in Chapter 4.

One caveat: My argument in this chapter has been that *after* developing its strategy, a firm must design the organizational environment that supports it. It is often argued that such neat and tidy thinking misrepresents what is in reality a much more problematic and difficult process. In this view, a company cannot simply throw away its existing culture, structure, incentives, and people in order to build new ones that will support its new strategy. Its existing organizational environment is a constraint that must be taken into account.

There is of course some truth in this argument, but the message to take away from it is that a company *should* take its existing organizational environment into account when developing a new strategy. This way, the "new" strategy will reflect the ongoing realities of the company. For example, if the company finds that an aspect of its existing culture will not allow proper implementation of the strategy it hopes to pursue, then it has a choice to make: either abandon the idea of changing the strategy in the way it is being proposed (since it cannot be implemented), or consider how the organizational environment might be changed to support the new strategy. Either way, the company will have examined its existing organizational environment at the strategy formulation stage.

When Changes Outside the Firm Call for Changes Within

No matter how much flexibility you may have embedded in your organizational environment, the day will come when you will have to fundamentally change or abandon it. Remember that the organizational environment aims to support and promote the firm's chosen strategy. The strategy, in turn, aims to achieve fit between the firm and its external environment. If the external environment changes, the strategy needs to change as well—thus necessitating a shift in the underlying organizational environment.[10] If the strategy is changed without a corresponding change in the underlying environment, the new strategy will fail.

Remember People Express? Its entire organizational environment was designed to support a young entrepreneurial company in pursuit of a low-cost strategy. Its culture was open-door, entrepreneurial, and team oriented. Decisions were made by committee, and everyone was involved in the deliberations. Its structure was essentially flat, with minimal hierarchy, no specialization, much cross-utilization and transfer of people, and a lot of self-management. Its incentives emphasized lifelong job security, personal growth, and stock options. Its people were young and ambitious, and they were carefully selected from hundreds of applicants.

This organizational environment served the young, entrepreneurial firm well. However, by 1985, the company had grown from zero to $1 billion in revenues. At that stage, it needed an organizational environment that could support a mature and professional billion-dollar corporation. By failing to put this supporting infrastructure in place, People Express declined into bankruptcy by 1986.

Its failure to change its organizational environment was expressed well in a 1986 story in the *Wall Street Journal*:

> The airline's operations have deteriorated badly, leaving many travelers in the lurch. Flights are being overbooked by huge margins, bags are being lost by the thousands, passengers complain that bargain fares are boosted unexpectedly, and planes are chronically late. . . . The airline's meteoric growth has outstripped computer systems, baggage-handling systems and just about every other system needed to run it smoothly. Industry executives also say that fast growth is revealing flaws in People's basic strategies, flaws that are causing the service breakdowns . . . [the CEO's] abhorrence of bureaucracy and insistence on a loose management style may be more suited to a small, fledgling airline than one pushing rapid growth. People, a former worker says, "has too many Indians and not enough chiefs, and the result can be chaotic."[11]

In hindsight it is easy to criticize People Express for failing to create the new organizational environment it needed. But the problem that companies like People face is not a simple matter of recognizing the need to change and then simply changing. The problem is to recognize the need; to identify the new culture, structure, incentives, and people that will be needed; to develop those four new elements; and to put them together in such a way that they once again fit and reinforce both each other and the new strategy. Needless to say, this is a hard trick to pull off. Still tougher is having to pull it off within the short time span generally available to rapidly growing companies such as People Express. Nevertheless, it must happen.[12] Recognizing the problems and dangers involved does not relieve the firm of its need to realign its organizational environment to fit and support a new strategy.

Leclerc is an example of a company that has built into its organizational environment the capacity and the flexibility to adapt to changes in the market and its strategy. The organization is a loose federation of more than 500 supermarkets spread throughout France and Europe. Decision making at Leclerc is decentralized, with the manager of each store having complete autonomy to manage that store's affairs appropriately for its competitive environment. This allows the organization to identify early and react quickly to environmental changes. It also allows for local entrepreneurship and innovation. Moreover, each store is owned by its store manager, and in each store 25 percent of the profits every year are distributed among the employees. This promotes a sense of ownership and belonging that translates into loyalty, willingness to work hard, and deep commitment to the organization.

The store owners continually reinforce Leclerc's culture of experimentation and caring. They regularly experiment with new products and formats for their individual stores while spending at least one day a week on the "common good"—that is, attending regional and national meetings, managing the regional warehouses for no extra pay, and selecting individuals from their stores whom they will "mentor" so that they can in due course set up their own Leclerc stores.

Overall, this kind of environment is characterized by entrepreneurship, a sense of belonging, teamwork, and fast and efficient response. As explained in Chapter 4, Leclerc achieved all this without sacrificing the benefits of size. The company has developed several mechanisms that allow individual stores to reap the benefits of large scale and scope.

The glue that holds Leclerc together is a powerful sense of direction that sets the parameters within which people operate. Even though every store has its individual personality, there is a larger "Leclerc culture" that permeates the organization. This culture supports the idea that "we" at Leclerc are different from everybody else: unlike other companies, "we" have a sense of destiny that goes beyond making money, and "we" have a way of doing things that combines individual values with the strength of the institution of family. As a result, "we" work together and help each other to achieve our goals, thus proving to the world that our way of doing things is better.

Leclerc has developed an organizational environment that enables it to achieve fit with its current strategy while remaining flexible to change. In its own unique way, every organization must do the same.

Summary

1. In a very real sense, an organization's underlying environment is what creates its employees' behavior. Therefore, to obtain the de-

sired behavior from employees, the firm must ensure that its environment is conducive to that behavior. This is crucial to the successful implementation of any new strategy. The organization must create an environment that will promote and support the behaviors needed to implement the new strategy properly.

2. The environment of an organization is composed of four elements: culture, structure, incentives, and people.

3. The challenge is to combine those elements in such a way that they support and reinforce one another while also supporting the firm's chosen strategy.

4. A change in the market necessitates a change in strategy, and a change in strategy will most likely necessitate a change in the organizational environment. The firm must be willing and ready to adapt.

7

Develop a Superior Strategic Position

Strategists may have a lot to say about the context and content of strategy, but they have, in recent years, had precious little to say about the conduct of strategy—[that is], the task of strategy-making. No one seems to know anything about how to create strategy. Managers today know how to embed quality disciplines, how to re-engineer processes and how to reduce cycle times, but don't know how to create new, innovative, wealth-creating strategies.

—Gary Hamel, "The Search for Strategy"

In hindsight, IKEA's positioning is indeed brilliant and is indeed a source of real and sustainable differentiation. The position, however, was as much a consequence of adaptability as it was of strategy. . . . Defensible strategies seldom emerge from analysis . . . [and] it is one thing to admire a company's positioning ex post facto. It is another to recognize it as one of a whole population of positions, including those that never made it.

—Ian C. MacMillan and Rita Gunther McGrath, letter to the *Harvard Business Review*

Thus far I have argued that a company must develop its strategy by finding answers to the questions "Who should we target as customers, what should we offer them, and how should we go about it?" Any company engaged in strategy making must raise these questions, identify possible answers, evaluate the answers, and make a choice. The objective should be to come up with ideas that differentiate the firm from its competitors. Therefore, the more creative the ideas, the better.

The challenge for any firm, then, is to use its strategy-making process so as to consistently come up with innovative ideas on how to compete in its industry. How can this be done? Do creative new strategies emerge from planning, or is something else involved here?

Consider again the case of Nespresso. There is no question that the strategy adopted by Jean-Paul Gaillard was a winning one. By targeting households instead of offices as his customers, by unbundling the coffee machines and their servicing from the sale of coffee, by developing two separate selling and distribution methods (one for the coffee and one for the machines), and by developing an aura of exclusivity through the Nespresso Club, Gaillard rejuvenated Nespresso, turning a dying operation into a growing unit for Nestlé.

But how did Gaillard come up with this strategy? Did he plan it all out to the last detail, or did the ideas somehow emerge over time through trial and error? According to Gaillard, it was a mixture of both. When he joined Nespresso, it was clear that the existing strategy was not working. Considering the situation he inherited and using his past experience as a guide, he made certain decisions—such as the decision to change the targeted customer focus from offices to households and to separate the coffee from the machine side of operations. "I knew in my guts that these were the correct decisions," says Gaillard. "But you are not 100 percent sure. So you try them out in a limited way; and you learn as you go along."

Contrast this experience with the way Lan & Spar developed its successful strategy. How did Peter Schou conceive his ideas to target white-collar customers, offer a limited number of products at low prices, and reach customers through a direct-banking concept? Like Gaillard, Schou attributes his success to a blend of careful planning *and* trial and error. He explains:

> I have been in the banking industry since the age of 16. By the time I moved to Lan & Spar as the CEO, I had already thought about the issues and I had pretty much decided on the main elements of our new strategy. In fact, I had tested this concept in a limited way in my previous bank. However, I had to go slow at first. We had to try out some of these things first before rolling them out full scale.

Finally, consider the development of Edward Jones's successful strategy. According to John Bachmann, the organization was originally set up by Mr. Jones, Sr., to be a department store specializing in finance. However, Mr. Jones's son, Ted, "did not like big cities," Bachmann recalls. "He loved agriculture. He refused to set up business in the city, so he went to Mexico, Missouri, and set up shop there and then started traveling around selling commodities. . . . We soon evolved into a distribution network to sell mutual funds in rural America."

When Bachmann joined the firm in 1970, he decided that the "formula worked, so we had to codify it—not just run it opportunistically. We therefore cast a series of principles in stone and started operating according to these principles. . . . Then we made a mistake—we thought of the brokers as our customers." Out of this mistake (and the learning that came from it) evolved the current Jones strategy: to be a merchant (that is, an informed buyer) for the individual investor.

All three examples demonstrate a simple but powerful point: *The process of developing superior strategies is part planning and part trial and error, until you hit upon something that works.* Analysis and planning will not produce a full-fledged strategy ready for implementation, but they will help narrow the options. Experimentation should then follow on that limited set of options, out of which the final strategy will emerge.

Strategy making must encompass both elements: planning and trial and error. This point can't be emphasized enough, because it has become popular for people to argue that in today's volatile environment, planning is useless. By the time you establish a plan, the claim goes, the environment has changed so much that your plan is no longer valid. The best you can do is develop an organizational environment that allows superior ideas and strategies to emerge from anyone and everyone in the organization as part of "standard operating procedures." I argue that this is not enough. A company that relies only on trial and error to develop its strategy is like a ship at sea with a rudder but no intended destination; it can go anywhere it wants, but it doesn't know where it wants to go.

The parameters within which the firm will operate must be developed before experimentation is allowed to take place; and, as mentioned earlier in the book, these parameters can be developed only by top management. There have been many calls lately to make the process of strategy development "democratic" and "flexible"—to bring everyone in the organization into the process.[1] The thinking here is that the odds of conceiving truly innovative ideas are increased if thousands of people rather than just five or six senior managers put their minds to the task. And this much is true. But the job of choosing the ideas the firm will actually pursue must be left to top management. Otherwise the result is chaos, confusion, and, ultimately, a demotivated workforce. After all is said and done, it is the leaders of the organization, not every single employee, who must decide which ideas will be pursued.

Therefore, to repeat my main point, the ideas that make up a strategy (such as what customers to target or what products to sell) can emerge through careful planning or after experimentation. Anybody in the organization can come up with these ideas, but it is the responsibility of top management to decide what will be implemented.

No matter how the ideas are conceived, it is unlikely that they will be perfect from the start. The firm must therefore be willing and ready to modify or change its strategic ideas as it receives feedback from the market. Nothing illustrates this point better than the example of IKEA, the Swedish furnishings company, as it went through the process of developing its successful strategy. Many of Ingvar Kamprad's original ideas were resisted by his Swedish competitors, who used their industry association and their political connections to sabotage his early plans. But he managed to outsmart them all by adjusting his strategy as he went along:

> When Ingvar Kamprad, IKEA's founder, tried to crack this market, he was shut out at every turn. Barred from selling directly at trade fairs, he resorted to taking orders there. When that was forbidden, he contacted customers directly (initiating a profitable mail-order business, which necessitated that the furniture be easy to ship). When Swedish manufacturers refused his business, Kamprad sourced from Poland, getting even better prices than before. Locked out of traditional outlets, Kamprad converted a factory into a warehouse and showroom, where explanatory tags, self-service, a colorful catalog, and the lure of instant availability—thanks to on-site stocking—were deliberately distinctive.

In every instance, the strategy was driven as much by necessity as it was choice. . . . In hindsight, IKEA's positioning is indeed brilliant and is indeed a source of real and sustainable differentiation. The position, however, was as much a consequence of adaptability as it was of strategy. It was persistence—and experimentation under the strict discipline imposed by constrained resources—that allowed IKEA to build its furniture franchise.[2]

To sum up my argument to this point: the creation of a new strategy involves two basic tasks (see Exhibit 7-1):

1. Generate as many ideas as possible on who to target, what to sell, and how to do it. These ideas can be generated through formal planning or trial and error and can come from anyone, anywhere, anytime.

2. Evaluate these ideas and choose which one(s) to put into action. Ideas can be evaluated either through a detailed cost-benefit analysis or, to see if they really work as intended, through market tests and experimentation. Depending on how the selected ideas fare in the market, modify them or change them altogether. Repeat the process.

It should be clear that experimentation, or trial and error, is used for two separate purposes: to generate new ideas and to test and evaluate these ideas. It should also be clear that at the generation-of-ideas stage, numerous tactics can be used to maximize the number of ideas generated; holding a formal strategic planning session is only one. Finally, note that the process is not unidirectional. At any stage, you can either return to the previous stage or move on to the next. The evaluation/experimentation/learning/modifying cycle continues until a unique set of activities that defines a unique position—that is, a new strategy—emerges.

Generate Ideas

A firm can generate innovative strategic ideas in any number of ways. A formal planning process, which is the easiest for the firm to employ, will be discussed shortly. The following is an example of a more democratic approach to idea generation.

Ideas from Anybody, Anywhere, Anytime

Given the right environment, strategic ideas can be conceived by anybody, anywhere, anytime. The key word here is *environment*, as in *organizational environment*—the culture, structure, incentives, and people that promote and encourage the generation of ideas, as described in Chapter 6. In this kind of environment, new ideas can bubble up throughout the organization. The greater challenge is to get these ideas to the decision makers. For that, the company needs a process that will enable it to (1) pick up the ideas quickly, (2) bring them to the attention of decision makers quickly, (3) allow for a fair and transparent evaluation of the ideas, and (4) put the ideas to the test. A look at one such process, adopted by

Exhibit 7-1   The Creation of a New Strategy

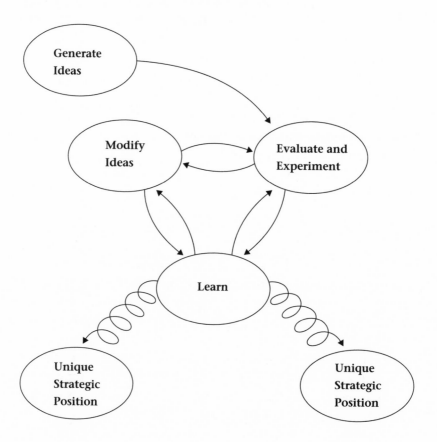

Schlumberger, a multinational corporation that operates in oil-field services, measurement and systems, and communication and information technology solutions, is instructive.

In 1994, Schlumberger set up an internal venture unit to promote innovation in the company and to ensure that "unexploited" opportunities that did not fit comfortably within existing business units got a fair hearing from top management. According to Robert Davis, who heads the unit, the need for it became evident despite the fact that Schlumberger was (and is) a very entrepreneurial and innovative organization:

> In this company, it's career-enhancing to be innovative, and our people are able to stand up and criticize the system without being shot. Our culture is to shake up the company, to remake it continuously even if it is working well. Still, a lot of ideas and opportunities fall through the cracks. We needed a formal way to look at the big picture.

The internal venture unit solicits ideas on an annual basis from the business units. The ideas must lie *outside* the domain of the business units (ideas within the jurisdiction of a business unit should be handled by the business itself). Ideas that deal with issues or areas that do not usually get enough management attention are also given priority. The internal venture unit evaluates these ideas and selects those which it believes deserve further attention. Bob Davis sees the role of the unit as follows:

> We are *not* gatekeepers but advisors. We want to encourage this kind of behavior so we don't crush ideas. We work with the proposer to think it through, and we challenge them to clarify what they want to do. We also help them package their ideas so as to present them to top management.

If an idea passes this initial evaluation stage, then the employee championing the product needs to be provided with the time and resources necessary to develop it further. "His current job may suffer as a result," says Davis. "His managers know this but are willing to turn a blind eye. The divisional manager has profit-loss responsibility but is still expected to support an entrepreneur in his division. It is good citizenship to do so." The internal venture unit lobbies division managers to support the entrepreneurs in their midst. The unit also can allocate financial resources from its budget.

Once the idea passes this early experimentation stage, it is assigned to a separate project team that has its own space and resources. This team must develop a business plan to present to top management. But even here, the internal venture unit plays a crucial role, Davis says.

> We spend a lot of time selling the project to all the executive VPs. By the time it gets to a formal presentation, it is a sold project. Because most of the product champions do not have access to the corporate [center], we act as their brokers. We have a lot of personal relationships and we use them.

How successful has the internal venture unit been? Several measures indicate that it has done quite well. Within its first three years the unit can claim the successful commercialization of one venture (the software firm Global Soft), and a few more ideas are at various stages of development. Another indicator of the unit's success is the number of ideas nominated every year. According to Davis: "We now get so many ideas, we don't solicit them any more!" Finally, if imitation is an indicator of success, the unit can be very proud of itself. Several business divisions within Schlumberger are developing their own internal venturing units. "Little clones of us are now developing in the business units," Davis says.

Ideas through Formal Strategic Planning

Recall how Ingvar Kamprad came up with all the wonderful ideas that allowed IKEA to create a unique position for itself in the home furnishings market. Most of those ideas were responses to problems. He tried something. Whether or not it worked, he learned something from the experience, applied this learning to another idea, and experimented again. Eventually he emerged from this process of trial and error with a unique set of activities that defined a unique and successful position for IKEA. Most managers will relate to this story because this is exactly how they come up with new ideas—that is, in response to problems. Another way to generate new strategic ideas is through planning. Although formal strategic planning has received a lot of bad publicity lately, it should not be dismissed too quickly. Done properly, planning can be an effective way for an organization to challenge its assumptions and beliefs and generate innovative new ideas.

Challenge your assumptions and beliefs. The primary objective of a planning session should be to revisit the questions of who/what/how and "what business are we in?" and to challenge the answers the company arrived at in previous planning sessions. If the objective is to find innovative answers to these fundamental questions, creativity and active, innovative thinking will make all the difference.

How can a company maximize creativity at this stage? Throughout this book, I have emphasized the importance of looking at the four "big" questions creatively and of continually challenging prior answers to them. I have also suggested that involving all employees in generating ideas can produce quite a few new and innovative ideas. In Chapters 2–4, I specifically identified the following four tactics as effective *during* a strategy planning process:

1. Proactively question the answer that a company's managers (or its managers before them) gave to the question "what business are we really in?" This questioning should enable you to redefine your business in a way that allows you to maximize the impact of your unique capabilities relative to your competitors. We discussed how to do this in detail in Chapter 2.

2. Redefine the *who*. Proactively question who your customers really are and try either to identify new customers or to resegment the existing customer base in a more creative way and thus create new customer segments. This should lead to the development of a new game plan for serving these customers better. We discussed this tactic in detail in Chapter 3.

3. Redefine the *what*. Proactively question what is your company's real value-added and what you are really offering to customers. This should allow you to identify new or changing customer needs or priorities, thereby helping your firm to be the first in its market to develop new products and services that will better satisfy customer needs. We discussed this tactic in detail in Chapter 3.

4. Redefine the *how*. Question the way in which your firm delivers value to its customers, the way it is playing the game. By exploiting core competencies, you should be able to identify more profitable ways of selling or distributing or manufacturing or playing the game in general. We discussed this tactic in detail in Chapter 4.

These four tactics are more useful and relevant to an established firm than to an entrepreneurial start-up. The more open-minded the organization is in questioning its accepted answers, the higher the likelihood that it will come up with new ideas. Thus, having the right attitude going into the process is as important as the process itself.

Start the process at different points. Another way of facilitating active thinking during a planning session, also mentioned earlier in the book, is to start thinking from different points in the process. For example, instead of thinking, "This is my customer, this is what he or she wants, and this is how I can offer it," you might ask, "What are my unique capabilities, what specific customer needs can I satisfy with these capabilities, and who will be the 'right' customer to approach?"

Entering the process at a different point can be very effective in promoting innovative thinking because it allows you to sidestep your company's dominant way of thinking. For example, some companies may start with their customers and try to determine what products or services to offer them. Other companies typically start with their core competencies and seek ways of leveraging them. And so on. Different companies have different dominant ways of thinking. There is no right or wrong way to do it, but the more a company is able to "escape" its dominant way of thinking and try new approaches, the greater its chances of being innovative.

There are six possible ways a company can approach the who/what/how question:

1. who/what/how

2. who/how/what

3. what/who/how

4. what/how/who

5. how/what/who

6. how/who/what

The three most popular approaches above are numbers 1, 3, and 5. In the first approach the firm decides *who* to target, then determines *what* to offer and *how* to do it. In approach 3, the firm starts the process by deciding *what* products or services it will offer; based on this decision, it determines *who* will want to buy these products and *how* it will produce and deliver them. In approach 5, the firm begins with its existing core competencies (*how*) and, based on these competencies, decides *what* products and services to offer and *who* is likely to buy them.

There is no one correct way to think through the issues. Any attempt to create strategy must force managers to utilize as many of the above-mentioned approaches as possible. One way to get the management team to look at these issues in new ways is to take it through a number of exercises, all of which tackle the same issue but from different angles. For example:

Exercise 1: Identify the problems you are currently facing. Given these problems, what actions do you think you should be taking?

Exercise 2: Identify your current core competencies. How can you leverage these competencies in new products or new markets? What new competencies will you need to develop in the future?

Exercise 3: Identify the changes taking place in your industry. Given these changes, how should you respond? Can you see any new customer segments emerging that you should be targeting? Can you see any new customer needs that you should aim to satisfy?

Exercise 4: What criteria would you use to decide whether a customer is "right" or "wrong" for the firm (according to the definitions discussed in Chapter 3)? Apply these criteria to determine which customers you want to target and decide how to target them.

Exercise 5: What business are you really in? Can you think of any other possible definitions for your business? Explore the implications of defining your business in the different ways you have identified.

Exercise 6: What are the key success factors in your business? How are they changing? How should you respond to these changes?

Exercise 7: What is your real value-added? Why do customers buy from you? Why do they buy from your competitors? Given the changes taking place in your industry, what will be your value-added in the future?

Exercise 8: Who do you consider to be your most threatening competitors? How are they playing the game? What would your firm have to do to outdo its chief competitors?

While the above questions are ostensibly to be asked of the management team, they can also be put to other employees. Again, the more people and the more diverse the people who are asked to think about these questions, the better the outcome. For example, the use of strategy workbooks has encouraged Lan & Spar employees to contribute their ideas for improving some aspect of the business, which has created a huge database of ideas for the bank to evaluate and test.

Evaluate, Experiment, Learn, Modify

Once new ideas have been generated, they have to be evaluated in a fair yet rigorous way and put to the test of implementation. The firm must then step back to assess the results of its "experiment," to learn from its successes and failures and put its learning to work in improving those ideas.

Evaluate

It is crucial to draw a clear line between the stage of generating ideas and that of evaluating them. Without such a distinction, people often start to criticize a new idea the moment it is proposed.

This can have a chilling effect on the entire process of idea generation, discouraging people who might otherwise have contributed. Generation is not the same as evaluation, and every effort must be made to keep the two separate.

It is neither possible nor advisable for a company to implement every proposed idea, but it is imperative for people to understand why their specific ideas have not been selected. This means that every company must have clear and explicit evaluation criteria. In addition, as mentioned earlier, the evaluation and selection process must be transparent and perceived as fair. It is the responsibility of the CEO to explain which ideas have been selected and why, and which ideas have been rejected and why.

New ideas can be evaluated along numerous criteria. Prominent among them are the following:

- Does the idea reinforce the organizational vision?

- Does the idea "fit" within the necessary parameters established by the business the company is in?

- Would the idea have a significant impact on the bottom line?

- Does the idea build on core competencies?

- Is there enough emotional support for the idea?

- Are there sufficient resources and capabilities to implement the idea?

Experiment, Learn, and Modify

Most of the time, an idea cannot be evaluated with 100 percent certainty. This is where experimentation comes in: by actually implementing the idea in a limited way, you can learn whether or not it works and under what circumstances. You can then take that experience into account (learn from it) in deciding where to take the project next.

Two requirements must be met if such experimentation is to succeed: First, the organization must develop the kind of culture and environment that encourage innovation, generation of new ideas, and experimentation. Second, the organization must ensure that learning comes out of the experience and that this learning permeates the organization. To achieve this end, it needs to develop a learning culture and build structures and processes that facilitate and promote learning.

Experimenting with new strategic ideas can be both exhilarating and demanding. The following explains how to deal with some of the more common challenges you may face as you experiment with new ideas.

The challenge of uncertainty. Early on, a lot of uncertainty surrounds the new idea. You don't know who the customer will be, whether the market will develop, what the final product will look like, or how you should sell it and distribute it, so you cannot rely on conventional marketing techniques. These techniques tend to focus on existing customers, whereas the idea being tested may be intended for totally different customers. For example, when Motorola developed the mobile phone, the company thought that the users of the new product would be people who don't own a car or people who own several cars. As it turned out, the real market emerged from traveling salespeople.[3] Similarly, the manufacturers of 5.5 floppy disks thought that their customers would be the traditional computer manufacturers like IBM. But it was the PC manufacturers, such as Compaq and Dell, that saw the potential of the new product.

If you cannot rely on conventional marketing techniques to determine if the idea will be accepted by the market or who your customers will be, how can you manage all this uncertainty? The way successful innovators have done it is through an experimental approach to the market that academic researchers have labeled variously as discovery-driven planning, expeditionary marketing, and search and probe.[4] The process involves three steps:

1. Develop *early* (even immature) prototypes of the product or strategic idea.

2. Put these prototypes out in the market and test them in *several potential market segments*. For example, Corning tested its optical

fibers in four potential customer segments (long-distance phone, picture phone, cable TV, and military applications) before settling on long-distance phone lines as its market.[5] Similarly, Searle tested variants of its NutraSweet product in several potential customer segments (soft drinks, chewing gum, candy, table-top sweeteners) before settling on a few of these applications.[6] The purpose of such testing is *learning:* to learn about the technology and how to improve it, to learn about the needs of potential users, to learn whether a market exists or whether you need to develop a whole new market, to learn which product application interests which customer segment, to learn what problems emerge, to learn how sensitive the whole enterprise is to changes in government regulations, and so on.

3. Finally, use this accumulated learning to introduce improved versions of the product or the strategic idea in a more focused way, that is, through more appropriately targeted customer segments and through more focused and better marketing.

The challenge of inertia. Having resolved the problem of uncertainty, it is time to put the new strategic idea in the market and to promote it aggressively—to the right customers. But the company is already in business, selling its existing products (which embody a certain technology) to a set of existing customers. When a new idea calls for the firm to create new products or new ways of selling or distributing, it can't be assumed that *existing* customers will be interested in them. Remember that it is usually a new and totally different customer segment that adopts new technology and products. By focusing only on the needs and wants of your current customers, you continue to invest your resources in the products those customers want, thus ignoring or underinvesting in the new technology or product until it is too late.

A possible solution to this problem is to create a separate organizational unit dedicated to the new idea. The new unit can then allocate its resources specifically to attract the new customers that will want the new offering. Without the huge overhead costs of its parent company, the unit can make money and survive. Several examples of companies that created successful new units spring to mind: Midlands Bank in the United Kingdom set up its telephone banking unit, First Direct, as a stand-alone operation with profit-loss responsibility; Audi established a totally separate unit to develop and commercialize the aluminum car; Boston-based Thermo Electron Corp regularly spins out its new technologies into stand-alone entities; and 3M creates separate divisions for every product innovation that reaches a certain size.

The organizational challenge. A new technology or product, simply by virtue of being new, originally creates a small market that requires time to grow. A large corporation considering investing in such a small emerging market will likely find the prospect unappealing. At best the new market would make only a small contribution to its profitability. As a result, the new idea rarely receives the attention and resources it needs.

The tactic for dealing with this challenge is the same as that proposed for challenge 2, above: create a separate unit that is small enough to get excited about the new market. By separating it from the existing organization, you can save it from suffocation. The unit has dedicated people who consider the new idea "their baby" and who will therefore fight for it. According to Clayton Christensen, a professor at Harvard University, separating the new innovation from the existing organization has other benefits as well: the separate organization has cost structures that allow it to make money in the value network where the new technology is taking root, and it allows the customers' power to be aligned with the managers' intentions.[7]

A classic example of this tactic is provided by Thermo Electron, where promising businesses within the corporation are regularly spun off (or "spun out," the term Thermo Electron uses) as separate, publicly traded divisions. Although Thermo Electron keeps a majority stake in each of its spin-offs, it gives them far more autonomy and freedom than a typical subsidiary gets. The company now boasts twenty-two spin-offs (which include spin-offs of spin-offs).

According to the firm's CEO, George Hatsopoulos, the process can be a lengthy one:

> Typically, people start [these spin-offs] as research projects. When a project reaches a point where it needs substantial resources—say more than $100,000—senior management reviews it and decides whether to sup-

port it and how. We usually don't decide to set something up as a new division until we can see the shape of the business. That often takes several years or more. In the case of Thermo Cardiosystems, which developed a device that assists heart patients who are awaiting a transplant, it took more than 20 years of research supported by the federal government to get approval from the Food and Drug Administration. We have found that, despite the sometimes lengthy gestation period, the opportunity to have a business spun out goes a long way toward keeping employees motivated and focused.

For the investors, this approach has offered a means of participating in a particular technology as opposed to investing in the company as a whole. For the spun-out businesses themselves, it generally has provided an opportunity to raise equity to finance growth. And for employees and managers involved in the various spin-outs, it has provided a new vehicle for ownership. It has given them direct feedback about how their business is viewed by the market and a real incentive to increase its value.[8]

Sidestep the Traps of Strategy Making

Companies can get caught in a number of predictable traps as they go through the process of developing new strategies. A strategist needs to be aware of these traps to manage the process of strategic development properly. Failure to manage the process will result in half-baked ideas, a demoralized workforce, and a directionless organization. Below I describe a few of the traps likely to trip up strategy makers.

Stargazing. Most companies develop ambitious, stretching goals and then challenge their employees to shoot for them. But most of these goals are fruitless. What really distinguishes the successful strategic innovators is not the quality or the magnitude of the challenges they set for themselves but *the time and effort they spend selling those challenges to everyone throughout the firm.* Without emotional commitment, other strategy-making activities are a waste of time. People get excited and passionate about an organizational goal only if they believe in it—that is, only if they have "bought into it." How many companies do you know that spend the time and effort selling an organizational goal to their employees?

Strategy as analysis. Many strategic planners confuse the tools and frameworks of strategy with the strategy itself. In many companies, strategic planning takes the form of mindless number crunching and endless projections, the ultimate purpose of which is to prepare lengthy reports that no one will read. Instead, strategic planning should be a mixture of rational thought and creativity, of analysis and experimentation, of planning and learning. Effective strategic thinking is both creative and intuitive (not merely rational) and based on (but not supplanted by) analysis. It continually asks questions and works through issues in creative ways. Thus, correctly formulating the questions is often more important than finding a "solution," exploring an issue from a variety of angles is often more productive than collecting and analyzing unlimited data, and experimenting with new ideas is often more critical than conducting scientific analysis and discussion.

Analysis paralysis. It can be easier to ask for more information and to continue analyzing information than to make a firm decision. Choosing one course of action implies rejecting all others. For example, deciding to target customer X means not targeting customer Y, deciding to invest in country A means not investing in country B, and deciding to adopt distribution P means not adopting distribution Q. Such strategic choices are difficult to make, and they are always cause for internal debates. Managers find it easier to avoid making these choices by asking for more information and more analysis.

Emphasis on operational improvements. Managers are preoccupied with the question of how: How can we cut costs? How can we reengineer ourselves to become more customer-oriented? How can we speed up our new product development process? How can we empower our employees, better manage our supply chain, improve on product quality? Effective strategy development processes encourage managers to question the *who* and the *what* as well as the *how*. In fact, as I have argued in this book, innovation in strategy more often takes place when a company challenges the answers it has given to the questions of *who* and *what* rather than *how*.

Failure to choose. One of the most dangerous traps in the strategy-making process is the belief that making a particular choice will cause a firm to lose its flexibility. In choosing option XYZ, the argument goes, we tie our fortunes to XYZ; if it goes down, we go down with it. Better to keep our options open so we're ready to respond to whatever may happen. Yet the failure to make clear choices is *not* a recipe for flexibility—it is a recipe for disaster. As I argued in Chapter 4, a firm needs to make tough choices while remaining flexible enough to respond to changes in the outside environment. *The failure to choose is one of the cardinal sins in strategy.*

Failure to revisit the strategy every year. Designing a successful strategy is a never-ending quest. The fact that Dell and Wal-Mart have superior strategies and are successful today is no guarantee that they will be successful tomorrow. Tomorrow's success requires a superior strategy for tomorrow's market. An effective strategic process, then, must encourage firms to think about tomorrow's market and to develop a strategy for success in those markets—not in the markets of today. Whatever decisions have been made in any given year must be revisited and questioned in subsequent years.

Summary

1. The creation of a new strategy is part planning and part trial and error. Planning is necessary to define the parameters within which experimentation can take place.

2. The process of strategy creation consists essentially of two parts: (1) generation of ideas and (2) evaluation, experimentation, learning, and modification. This second aspect of the process may continue through many cycles until the firm arrives at a strategy that gives it a unique market position.

3. New strategic ideas can be generated in a variety of ways. Continually questioning the way the firm currently does business is one. Planning is another.

4. New strategic ideas must reach decision makers quickly and must be evaluated in a fair and transparent way. A company must develop processes that allow for this to happen.

5. The strategy-making process can be derailed in a number of ways. Care must be taken to avoid these traps of strategy making.

PART II

How to Prepare for Strategic Innovation

To be successful, a company must create and exploit a truly unique strategic position in its industry, in the manner described in Part I. However, no position will remain unique or attractive forever. Not only do competitors imitate attractive positions but also—and perhaps more important—*new* strategic positions continually emerge in every industry. These new positions have the potential to grow and challenge the existing ones for supremacy in the industry. Notice what's happening to Barnes & Noble with the arrival of Amazon.com and on-line retailing, and to Merrill Lynch as on-line brokerage continues to grow. Remember also how Canon attacked Xerox by creating a new strategic position in the copier business and growing that position at the expense of Xerox's position.

New positions (which are nothing more than new, viable who/what/how combinations) emerge in every industry as a result of evolving industry conditions, new technologies, and changing customer needs and preferences. Most of the time, these positions maintain themselves as small niches on the periphery of the mass market. But every so often, one of them grows and captures a significant share of the market. One problem for established competitors is figuring out which of these many new positions will fall into the second category—that of strategic innovation. Another is figuring out what to do once a likely candidate has been identified:

should they ignore it and focus on their existing position or should they try to colonize the new position as well?

The three chapters in this second part of the book address these two challenges. While there are systematic approaches that every firm can use to address them, there is no one right answer, or strategy, for all firms. Each must take its particular circumstances into account to develop a successful response to strategic innovation.

Of course, the emergence of a new strategic position in the industry is not the only threat that a firm might face. Many possible events may occur in a company's future (such as deregulation, industry maturity, globalization, and the like), which means that as part of every strategy process, a company must always ask: "What if this or that event happened? What should I be doing to prepare for it?" It also means that a company ought to remain flexible, in the manner described in Chapter 4. The next three chapters focus specifically on the threat of strategic innovation and discuss how a firm might respond to such a threat.

8

Understand How New Strategic Positions Develop

This is a dying business and very few of the people involved want to admit that the patient is sick. . . . Everybody's going after the same writers, the same concepts, the same audience. They're programming themselves out of business.

—Senior TV executive, quoted in *Fortune*, 12 January 1998

Every day the world turns upside down on someone who thought they were sitting on top of it.

—Glen Tullman, President, CCC Information Services

So far, I have argued that strategy is all about asking the who/what/how questions, generating possible answers, and then selecting specific ideas to put into action. Since different companies answer these questions in different ways, different strategies emerge, even in the same industry. The choices companies make at any given time position them in a specific location on what I call their industry's strategy positioning map, as shown in Exhibit 8-1.

Consider, for example, the automobile business. Within this industry, BMW has identified several customer segments to focus on and offers a number of product models accordingly. Porsche, meanwhile, has targeted a primarily different customer segment (with some overlap with BMW segments) and offers these customers a different range of product attributes. In contrast, Honda has targeted another set of customer segments and offers a different set of products. Honda's positioning is very similar (though not identical) to that of Ford in the same way that the positioning of Mercedes resembles that of BMW.

The various car companies have come up with different answers to the who/what/how questions and have therefore taken different positions on the strategy positioning map. This does not mean that any one position is better than the others. Nor does it mean that the companies are stuck with their choices forever; any company can decide to change its customer orientation or product offering at any given time. Doing so may be difficult, but it is not impossible.

Playing the Same Game, Only Better

Over time, the strategy positioning map of any industry tends to fill up. This means that most potential customer segments have been defined and are being served, most possible products and services are being offered in one form or another, and most possible distribution or manufacturing methods or technologies are being utilized. Once the potential for finding unexploited who/what/

Exhibit 8-1 The Strategy Positioning Map of an Industry

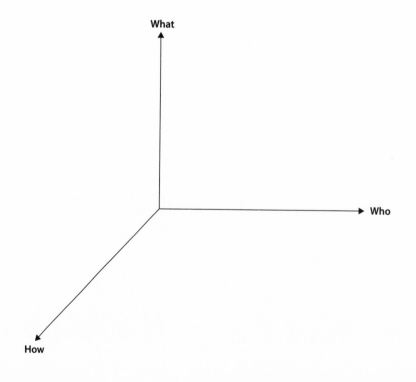

how positions in the industry space has been exhausted, companies shift their attention to making operational improvements—that is, they invest their resources in improving their "value-for-money" proposition to entice customers away from their rivals. This shift in the nature of competition leads to aggressive rivalry in the business, which eventually degenerates into pure price competition, at which point no competitor makes much money.

Making this shift to operational improvements in existing positions is nonetheless absolutely necessary. Simply finding a unique who/what/how position on the strategic map does not protect a firm from competition. For example, Dell has staked out a unique position in the PC business. So has Enterprise Rent-A-Car in the car rental business, Edward Jones in the brokerage business, and Southwest in the airline business. Yet, Dell is in competition with IBM and Compaq, Enterprise with Hertz and Avis, Edward Jones with Merrill Lynch and Smith Barney, Southwest with Delta and American. Unique positions do not isolate these firms from competition. Each must still strive to improve its customer offerings through better value-for-money propositions—or risk losing customers to its competitors.

While striving to improve its current position through operational improvements, a company must also try to protect that position from imitators. But such protection need not be derived from barriers to entry or government legislation. Rather, a firm can protect its position by doing two things:

1. *Organizing its activities into a tight system such that they support and reinforce one another.* As argued in Chapter 4, by building a "mosaic" of self-reinforcing activities, a firm makes it difficult for competitors to imitate its position; they must not only imitate the individual activities but the interactive "mosaic" as well.

2. *Creating an underlying organizational environment that supports the strategic position.* As argued in Chapter 6, every strategy requires the support of a certain organizational environment—the firm's culture, structure, incentives, and people. For a competitor to imitate a firm's strategic position, it must also imitate the underlying environment. A firm with a tightly knit environment that strongly supports its strategy will be difficult for competitors to imitate.

Changing the Rules of the Game

While established competitors try to outdo one another in their existing positions, strategic innovators build their success by discovering and exploiting *new* strategic positions that emerge from time to time as the industry evolves. Consider, for example, the following list of companies:

- The Body Shop
- CNN
- Dell
- Direct Line Insurance
- easyJet
- Enterprise Rent-A-Car
- E-Trade
- Federal Express
- First Direct
- Home Depot
- IKEA
- MTV
- Nucor
- OM Exchange (Sweden)
- Southwest Airlines
- Starbucks
- Swatch
- Timex
- *USA Today*

All of these companies are now household names. What distinguishes them from other well-known companies is the relatively short time in which they achieved global fame and fortune—in the face of formidable, entrenched competitors and without the benefit of a technological innovation.

In most industries, competitors fight it out among themselves, often spending billions of dollars in advertising or price wars, with very little to show for their efforts. Despite the enormous expenditures on these competitive battles, competitors often see only *marginal* fluctuations in their market shares. Throughout the fray, market share typically vacillates among the competitors, and one competitor may end up with a 1 or 2 percent improvement in its position. Rarely does a company carve out a significant slice of the market, and still more rarely in just five or ten years. Yet the companies listed above have done exactly this.

The enormity of their achievement becomes even clearer when compared with the track record of similar companies. Most of the companies listed above are new entrants in their respective markets. Statistics show that most new entrants in a business fail within five years,[1] and even those few which do not fail manage to capture only a small share of the market—about 5 percent in five years.[2] Again, my point is simple: not only have all the above-listed companies *not* failed in attacking the established leaders in their market, but they have succeeded in dramatically increasing their own market share and sometimes even emerged as the new industry leader. What's more, they accomplished this without utilizing a new technology. The question is, how did they do it?

After studying more than thirty such companies, I believe that the reason for their success is simple. Instead of attacking the established competitors in their existing, well-protected positions, these innovators created *new* strategic positions, which in turn allowed them to change the rules of the game by which everyone else in the market was playing. What is a *new* strategic position? Nothing more than a new who/what/how, or a new combination of these three:

1. *A new who*—that is, a new customer segment that is emerging because of changes in the industry, or an existing customer segment that other competitors have neglected, or even a segment that has been created from the existing customer base through more creative segmentation. For example, the innovation behind

the success of companies such as Canon and Apple Computers was the identification of "new" customer segments arising from changing consumer preferences and shifting industry conditions. The innovation behind the success of companies such as Enterprise Rent-A-Car and *USA Today* was the creation of "new" customer segments through more creative resegmentation of the existing customer base. And the innovation behind the success of companies such as Wal-Mart and Southwest Airlines was the exploitation of what appeared to be "new" customer segments—segments that other competitors were neglecting.

2. *A new what*—that is, the emergence of new customer needs or preferences as a result of changing demographics, or the identification of existing customer needs that are not being served well by other competitors. For example, "environmentalism" grew as a customer need over the last twenty years, and the Body Shop capitalized on it. CNN was the first television broadcaster to understand the business implications of the rapidly increasing number of Americans traveling abroad, and built its success on satisfying these consumers' need for news in English at their hotels. And Starbucks exploited a preference for tasteful, gourmet coffee that other companies in the business were not satisfying.

3. *A new how*—that is, a new way of producing, delivering, or distributing existing (or new) products/services to existing (or new) customer segments (usually but not always made possible by new technology). For example, Dell, Direct Line, E-Trade, and First Direct exploited new information technologies to create new distribution channels for their customers; Toyota revolutionized the car business by developing a new inventory system. Hanes (a subsidiary of Sara Lee) achieved enormous growth by developing a new selling and distribution method for its L'eggs pantyhose. And Nucor built its success in steel making by developing a new steel fabrication process.

Exhibit 8-2 sums up the sources of strategic innovation to be found in a new who, what, or how.

How do strategic innovators hit upon these masterstrokes? The companies we see as strategic innovators are *those companies which are the first to spot emerging strategic positions in the map of their industry.*

Exhibit 8-2   The Sources of Strategic Innovation

1. A new who
- a new customer segment that emerges from changes in the industry (such as shifting customer preferences or new demographics)

- a new customer segment created because the mass market is fragmenting

- a new customer segment formed by creative resegmentation of the existing customer base

- an existing customer segment that competitors have neglected

- an existing customer segment that "explodes" and grows enormously as a result of changes in the industry

2. A new what
- a new customer need that emerges from changes in the industry (such as shifting customer preferences or new demographics)

- a new customer preference becoming more important or "hot" as a result of changes in the industry

- a new customer need created by the marketing tactics of other companies

- an existing customer need that competitors have neglected

3. A new how
- a new way (usually made possible by a new technology) of manufacturing, distributing, selling, or delivering a new—or existing—product or service to a new—or existing—customer segment

---

They may even help to create these new positions. While the established competitors in the industry are busily competing with one another in their chosen positions, changing conditions (such as evolving industry conditions, changing customer needs and preferences, or newly discovered technologies) are giving rise to new customer segments, new products and services, or new ways of manufacturing or delivering the existing products. In short, changing external conditions produce new combinations of who/what/how. The established competitors, comfortable and happy in their existing territories, fail to notice these emerging positions. It is usually left to small and aggressive competitors (either new entrants or existing niche players) to recognize and go after these positions.

Why Strategic Innovation Isn't Easy
for Established Players

Most companies that become successful strategic innovators by identifying and exploiting new who/what/how positions in the market are small niche players or new market entrants. It is rare to see big, established competitors discovering new positions.

Established companies find it hard to become strategic innovators for numerous reasons. For example, established players already occupy a certain strategic position and may have difficulty escaping their mental models of who their customers really are and what they should be offering those customers. New or small companies, on the other hand, start with a clean slate and are therefore more likely to perceive emerging customer segments or needs. Similarly, established competitors already have a business position to take care of. If they are to strategically innovate, they may have to manage their existing position while simultaneously moving into a new strategic position—no easy task. Start-ups don't have this problem.

The obstacles to innovation grow even more formidable when a company's existing position is quite profitable and successful. Success in one position makes it very difficult, if not impossible, for a company to start searching for other positions. Unfortunately, success is almost always accompanied by numerous negative side effects, such as complacency, self-satisfaction, and managerial overconfidence or even arrogance (see Exhibit 8-3).

For a company even to begin to search for new strategic positions, let alone discover them, it must first overcome these barriers. In the next chapter, I describe how a company can deal with some of these problems and how it can approach the task of managing two positions at once, should it be innovative enough to discover a new strategic position.

Exhibit 8-3 The Negative Side Effects of Success

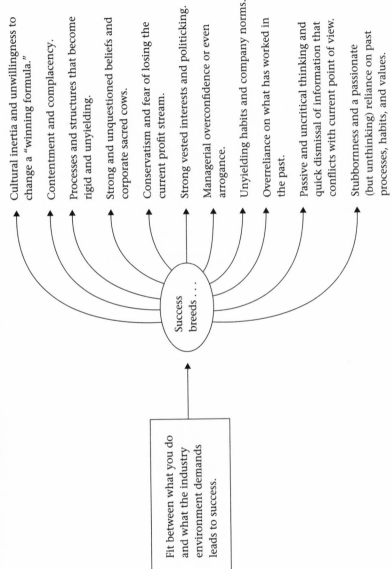

Fit between what you do and what the industry environment demands leads to success.

Success breeds . . .

Cultural inertia and unwillingness to change a "winning formula."

Contentment and complacency.

Processes and structures that become rigid and unyielding.

Strong and unquestioned beliefs and corporate sacred cows.

Conservatism and fear of losing the current profit stream.

Strong vested interests and politicking.

Managerial overconfidence or even arrogance.

Unyielding habits and company norms.

Overreliance on what has worked in the past.

Passive and uncritical thinking and quick dismissal of information that conflicts with current point of view.

Stubbornness and a passionate (but unthinking) reliance on past processes, habits, and values.

Summary

1. Once a company colonizes a unique position in its industry, it must try to improve it. Improving the company's position is absolutely essential in gaining advantage over competitors.

2. While improving its current position, the company must also be alert to new, potentially damaging positions that its competitors may be developing.

3. A new strategic position is simply a new, viable combination of who/what/how. To be considered a strategic innovation, a position must be new relative to existing positions and it must grow into a sizable market.

4. New strategic positions create conflicts for established competitors. In trying to exploit a new position, such a firm may jeopardize the viability of its existing position. This is probably the biggest problem established companies face in attempting strategic innovation.

9

Evaluate and Respond to Strategic Innovation

Typically, top management is pulled by two opposing, responsible forces: those that demand commitment to the old and those that advocate for the future. . . . Understanding and managing this tension perceptively may well separate the ultimate winners from the losers.

—James Utterback, *Mastering the Dynamics of Innovation*

The priest that tries to serve two churches cheats one of them.

—Greek proverb

This much is clear: the competitive landscape of every industry is always changing. Existing niches grow in size while others shrivel, new niches seem to be created out of thin air, the mass market fragments into all kinds of new segments (or niches), "old" niches merge to form larger markets, and so on. In this respect, the evolution of an industry resembles the evolution of the universe, as new stars are born, others die, still others collide and explode into millions of fragments, and others "merge," creating enormous black holes that suck in everything around them. In any industry, this dynamic is created by numerous forces, including changing customer preferences and needs, changing demographics, new technologies, changing government policies, and competitive moves and countermoves. Every organization in such a universe needs some guidance and navigation systems that will help it arrive at the choices it needs to make in order to find and then steer its course.

Imagine your company as it tries to navigate this ever-changing universe. You have already carved out a nice strategic position for yourself, but at any given time hundreds of new niches may be in the process of emerging around you. Most will fail. A few may survive. In certain cases, *one* of these newly created niches may grow into a sizable new market and come to be known as a strategic innovation. The trouble is, you don't know if this will happen, when it will happen, or how. Should your company explore the farther reaches of this universe—that is, seek out and deploy a strategic innovation of its own making? Or should it closely observe the changing scene, wait for other firms to experiment with new innovations, and then move in to exploit the one that is most likely to succeed? And, just as important, *when* should it act? Opportunities to act may present themselves all the time. The successful company will be judicious as it decides which opportunities to act on and when.

Evaluating Opportunities through Cost/Benefit Analysis

Suppose that your company has come up with an idea for a new strategic position—a strategic innovation. Or suppose that a new competitor has done so, and you immediately recognize its innovation as one that may influence your business. In both cases, your firm is faced with the same question: Should it pursue the innovation? The working assumption throughout this book has been that strategic innovation is the thing to do. In fact, it is not always the thing to do. A variety of factors should be considered before the decision to go ahead is made.

This point bears emphasis because the idea of strategic innovation has lately become very fashionable.[1] As the thinking now generally goes, all companies should become strategic revolutionaries, breaking the rules of the game in their respective industries. Yet for every company that has succeeded by breaking the rules, there are probably ten others that failed by doing so. For every Southwest Airlines there is a People Express, for every Compaq Computer an Osborne Computers, for every Virgin Atlantic a Kiwi International, for every Body Shop a Next Ltd. The corporate graveyard is littered with the corpses of companies that tried and failed to play by rules of their own making.

My goal here is not to scare you away from strategic innovation. Rather, I want to make clear that at any given point in time, a company has the option of playing a variety of games. Whether it should abandon its current game (that is, its current who/what/ how position) to adopt a new strategic position—even one that the company itself, rather than a competitor, has "discovered"—is not immediately obvious. The real issue for companies is not *whether* they should strategically innovate—urging companies to go out there and "just do it" is not smart advice. The real issue for thinking managers is: "*When* does it make sense for me to break the rules?" Only those executives who think through this question in a rigorous way will have a good chance of winning with strategic innovation. Going after whatever "hot" strategy of the month is being pushed by consultants and academics will not suffice.

Whether an individual company should break the rules depends on many factors, such as the nature of the industry, the nature of the game currently being played in the industry, the way value is created in the industry, the competitive position of the firm considering breaking the rules, and so on. These factors must be evaluated as they apply to each individual firm. After considering these factors, the firm may decide that for itself, it makes no sense to break the rules. In fact, among the top ten companies that according to *Fortune* magazine created the most wealth for their shareholders in 1996, only two could be considered rule breakers: Microsoft and Intel. The other eight companies (including number 1, Coca-Cola, and number 2, General Electric) created wealth by trying to be better than (not different from) their competitors. The same could be said for the 1997 *Fortune* list.[2]

If you are an entrepreneurial start-up (like the Body Shop or Dell Computers) or a new entrant into the business (like Canon, diversifying from cameras into the copier business, or, like the National Bank of Scotland, entering the insurance business), perhaps the best way to play the game is to break the rules. No sense trying to play the game the way the big established competitors in these businesses do; they have so many advantages that they will easily crush any new entrant that tries to play their game. In fact, all available evidence suggests that without the benefit of a new technological innovation, it is extremely difficult for any firm to successfully attack established industry leaders or to successfully enter a new market where established players exist. The strategy that seems to improve the odds of success in these situations is the strategy of breaking the rules.[3]

However, if you are an established industry player with a substantial market share position, you are facing a different situation. You have already taken your place on the who/what/how positioning map, and you are making a lot of money playing there. Suppose a new position is emerging. Should you abandon your current position for the new one? Alternatively, can you occupy both positions simultaneously?

Should American Airlines abandon its hub-and-spoke system and adopt the direct system of Southwest Airlines? Alternatively, can it play both games simultaneously?[4] Is that even possible? Similarly, should IBM give up on its extensive distribution channels of dealers and direct salespeople to move into the mail-order business, like Dell Computers? Alternatively, can it adopt the mail-order game while continuing to play its current game through its dealers? Or would this damage its relationships with the dealers?[5] Should Barclays Bank in the United Kingdom shut down its extensive branch network so as to follow Midlands Bank into telephone banking? Alternatively, can it organize itself to play both games efficiently? Should British Airways follow easyJet into the low-cost, low-price segment of the airline business?[6] Or will such a move damage its existing operations? Should Xerox have followed Canon into small copiers, selling them outright through dealers, or was it right to have stayed with its strategy of leasing big copiers through a direct sales force? Could it have played both games? Or would it have sacrificed too much from its existing game by attempting to play Canon's as well?

Clearly, the decision to rush into a new strategic position is not always the right one; in fact, Professor Michael Porter of Harvard Business School has forcefully argued against it.[7] He believes it is extremely difficult for a company to manage two strategic positions at once and that those who try to do it eventually fail. Everyone can't be a revolutionary. The decision whether to break the rules should be based on a detailed cost/benefit analysis: What are the *benefits* of embracing a new strategic position (and what are the costs of *not* embracing it)? What are the *costs* of embracing a new strategic position (and what are the benefits of *not* embracing it)? The relative benefits and costs depend on a number of factors.

Assessing the Benefits of Strategic Innovation

Many people assume that any strategic innovation will eventually grow to capture a large share of the market and deliver untold fortunes to its early adopters. This is far from certain. It could easily be an innovation that captures a small niche—period. If that is the case, you may be better off ignoring it and sticking to your existing game. If the innovation eventually catches on and begins to grow, you can then move in to take advantage of it (assuming you have the needed capabilities).

Of course, the problem lies in the fact that you don't really know if an innovation will grow or not, and, by waiting, you give your competitor a head start. By the time you decide to respond, it may be too late. This is in fact what happened to Xerox in the small copier market. As explained by John Seely Brown, corporate vice president at Xerox: "We had been late to recognize market opportunities for low- and mid-range copiers, and Japanese competitors like Canon were cutting into our market share."[8] As it turns out, Xerox assessed this new strategic position incorrectly. But just because this particular assessment was wrong does not take away from the fact that an assessment ought to be made in the first place before a new strategy is adopted. Thus, the decision whether or not to embrace an innovation should encompass your assessment of whether this innovation will catch on and grow or whether it will stay small. With luck, your assessment will be more accurate than Xerox's.

The benefits of a potential innovation are not determined solely by the size of the market you can capture with it. The innovation may indeed unlock a huge market for possible exploitation; the question is, "Can you exploit this market, given your current competencies and capabilities?" What makes an opportunity attractive is not only its intrinsic characteristics but also its fit with the strengths of your firm. Research shows that most established companies fail when attempting to adopt a new technological innovation that has invaded their market.[9] Among the reasons for their failure is their lack of the necessary core competencies to take advantage of the innovation. It's not possible to talk about "attractive" markets or customers in generic terms, and it's not possible to talk about strategic innovations in that way either.

The relative benefits of adopting a new strategic position will also be determined by your firm's current position in its existing business. Is the existing business mature or declining? Does that mean you can afford to divert investments elsewhere? Do you have a big stake in your current position, or a small one? Does that mean you could embrace the new position without losing too much ground in the existing one? These questions must be addressed if you are to make a correct assessment of the potential benefits of a strategic innovation.

An estimate of the benefits of adopting an innovation should also include costs that may accrue if you do *not* adopt it. For example, by not adopting an innovation, you may be giving a competitor the time and freedom to play the game at its own pace, to master it, and then to attack your primary business with that mastery. This is exactly what happened when Caterpillar spent some twenty years ignoring the "new" game that Komatsu had adopted in the earth-moving equipment business. Xerox made the same mistake, allowing Canon to develop the capabilities and resources to attack its primary business. Thus, even if you determine that pursuing a new strategic position would gain your firm little, you still might want to go after it to avoid the losses that could befall you from not acting.

Assessing the Costs of Strategic Innovation

Whatever your assessment of the benefits of a new strategic position, you must bear in mind that benefits represent only one side of the coin; you still have to assess the costs of adopting the position. Over and above the *direct costs* of actually competing in this new position, there are two other types of cost that should not be ignored: the cost to the existing business and the costs of complexity in trying to manage two, often conflicting, strategic positions.

First, there are the costs to the existing business. One such cost is the potential dilution of effort and investment in the current business for the sake of profits in the new position. Even if you possess the necessary competencies to compete in this new position, you must remember that no company can be all things to all customers. Sometimes the best course is to focus the firm's limited resources on a particular area. By trying to play both games, a company may weaken its efforts in both. Witness Kodak's difficulties in finding the right balance between its traditional film business and the new business of digital photography.

Another cost you can inadvertently inflict on your existing business is evidenced in the dilemmas that companies like IBM, Xerox, Unilever, and several insurance companies are facing as they consider adopting a distribution method that bypasses existing distributors. How will supermarkets—Unilever's traditional distribution outlets—react if Unilever tries to adopt another method of distribution, such as the Internet? Is it possible that grocery stores would threaten to stop selling Unilever products? And is this not a cost that Unilever ought to take into consideration in deciding whether to adopt the Internet as a method of distribution? Surely the answer to both of these questions is yes.

IBM confronted the same problem in trying to decide whether to follow Dell into the mail-order business. As Eric Beinhocker describes in his article "Strategy at the Edge of Chaos":

> When Dell Computer began to do well at selling inexpensive personal computers by mail, no doubt someone at IBM said, "Why don't we do that too?" But IBM could not follow suit without damaging its extensive distribution channels of dealers and direct salespeople. Its history and size created a tradeoff that Dell did not face and made it difficult for IBM to respond.[10]

This kind of cost must be entered into your cost/benefit equation.

A second type of cost associated with the adoption of a new strategic position is that of the complexity involved in trying to play two games simultaneously. As argued previously, you cannot simply "export" your current organizational setup and processes to the new strategic position and hope that all will be well. You will likely need to develop a completely new system to manage the new position—a new group of people, a new culture, new incentives, and so on. Starting and maintaining this system will have its costs, as will balancing the two (often conflicting) organizational infrastructures (as discussed further below). Witness the inability of most companies to achieve differentiation and low cost at the same time.

Trying to play two games simultaneously can also introduce damaging inconsistencies into the company's image or reputation. For example, in the mid-1980s, People Express acquired Frontier Airlines and tried to target businesspeople as customers. This move was in direct contrast with People's very strong image as a low-cost, no-frills airline. The company never managed to dispel that image, and businesspeople never accepted the new image that the acquisition of Frontier Airlines was meant to create. As a result, People Express went into bankruptcy.

Calculating the Cost/Benefit Equation

All of these factors should be entered into the cost/benefit equation in deciding whether to pursue a strategic innovation. But even if the decision is made to go ahead, the firm should not forget that this innovation can provide only temporary shelter. Eventually, more competitors will be attracted to this profitable who/what/how position. And, inevitably, the basis of competition will again shift from trying to be *different* to trying to be *better*. Listen, for example, to what a classic strategic innovator—Starbucks—is saying about how it will grow in the future. According to the company president, Orin Smith: "We're going to have to look more at opportunities to grow earnings, at how to manage the bottom line, not the top line. We're looking for efficiencies in manufacturing and distribution. We're reengineering."[11] In other words, Starbucks is now shifting its emphasis toward improving its strategic position.

The thinking process a company should go through in making decisions about strategic innovation appears in Exhibit 9-1. First and always, the firm must continue to question the basis of its existing business and the answers it gave a long time ago to the questions *who, what,* and *how*. It must continually search for new strategic positions. If it comes up with an idea for a new strategic position (or if it sees an outsider developing a new strategic position the firm may want to pursue), the firm must evaluate this new position to decide whether to adopt it. The evaluation process should follow the guidelines provided by the cost/benefit analysis.

Exhibit 9-1 How to Think about Strategic Innovation

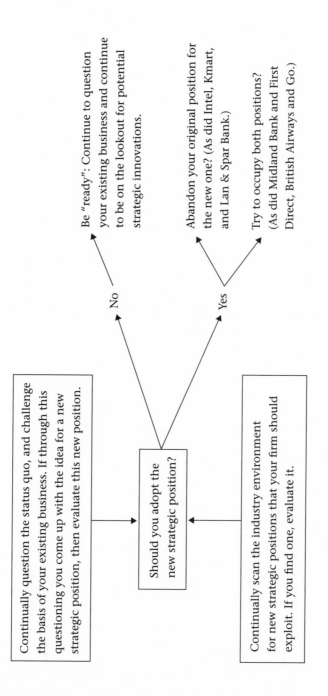

Continually question the status quo, and challenge the basis of your existing business. If through this questioning you come up with the idea for a new strategic position, then evaluate this new position.

Should you adopt the new strategic position?

Continually scan the industry environment for new strategic positions that your firm should exploit. If you find one, evaluate it.

No

Be "ready": Continue to question your existing business and continue to be on the lookout for potential strategic innovations.

Yes

Abandon your original position for the new one? (As did Intel, Kmart, and Lan & Spar Bank.)

Try to occupy both positions? (As did Midland Bank and First Direct, British Airways and Go.)

If the company decides not to adopt a potential strategic position, the firm must continue the questioning process so as to develop an idea for another innovation, and it must continue to scan the horizon for innovations it might exploit. It must also make itself ready (in the manner described in Chapter 4) to embrace an innovation should one appear on the horizon. If, on the other hand, the company decides to adopt the new position, it faces a dilemma: Should it abandon its current position and sink everything into the new one? Or should it try to occupy two positions simultaneously? If the latter, how?

Accommodating Opportunities: A Balancing Act of Old and New

In deciding to pursue a particular strategic innovation, the firm will need to determine how to continue competing effectively in its existing business while accommodating itself to the new one. Organizing the firm for a harmonious coexistence of the old and the new calls for the creation of an "ambidextrous" organization— a formidable assignment.[12]

As Michael Tushman and Charles O'Reilly point out, this ambidexterity "requires organizational and management skills to compete in a mature market (where cost, efficiency and incremental innovation are key) *and* to develop new products and services (where radical innovation, speed and flexibility are critical)."[13] In his book on technological innovation, James Utterback forcefully argues:

> Firms owe it to themselves to improve and extend the lives of profitable product lines. These represent important cash flows to the firm and links to existing customers. They provide the funds that will finance future products. At the same time, managers must not neglect pleas that advocate major commitments to new initiatives. Typically, top management is pulled by two opposing, responsible forces: those that demand commitment to the old and those that advocate for the future. Unfortunately, advocacy tends to overstate the market potential of new product lines and understate their costs. Management, then, must find the right balance between support for incremental improvements and commitments to new and unproven innovations. Under-

standing and managing this tension perceptively may well separate the ultimate winners from the losers.[14]

When a new strategic position emerges, the established players at first find it too small and too "problematic" to command their attention (recall the reasons Xerox delayed its response to Canon's discovery of a new strategic position). However, if over time the new position grows in size and attractiveness, it may become impossible for the established firms to ignore it. Witness the recent attempts by British Airways to move into the easyJet position in the U.K. airline business by forming a separate subsidiary called Go, and note the attempts by IBM, Compaq, and HP to move into Dell's direct-selling position. Even though these firms are aware of the many problems inherent in occupying two strategic positions simultaneously, the benefits of colonizing the ever-growing new position become too good to pass up. Under these conditions, established firms decide at least to try to occupy both positions.

The challenge for any established competitor is to organize itself so as to exploit the new position. Unlike a start-up firm, for which the new strategic position is the *only* position to occupy, the only game to play, the established firm has to play two games: trying to be *better* than its competitors in its existing business while at the same time trying to be *different* by moving into a new strategic position.

An example may help clarify this point. One of the biggest challenges facing consumer goods companies is the threat of generic (unbranded) products entering their markets. For example, major supermarkets are now offering their own brands of a variety of products, from cola drinks to soaps and detergents. These distributor-owned brands have made significant inroads in most European countries and in the United States, accounting for 20–50 percent of their respective markets. Their success is based on their recipe of good quality at cheap prices.

Established companies like Unilever must now decide whether to take the plunge and start offering their own "generic" products along with their more well-known brands. If they do decide to get into this business, they must re-examine the way in which they are organized. Unilever's organizational setup is geared toward innovation and the development of branded products: a certain culture and structure, incentives and people have been brought together and developed over the years to create an organizational environment that supports the strategy of differentiation. Generic (unbranded) products compete on the basis of price and require a low-cost strategy. This strategy will need the support of a totally different organizational environment. The question for Unilever is, how can it manage two different strategies and organizational environments at the same time?

Successful strategic innovators usually respond to this challenge by setting up a separate organizational unit—complete with its own culture, structure, incentives, and people—to support the new innovation. For example, Midland Bank set up its telephone banking unit—First Direct—as a totally different subsidiary. Similarly, Direct Insurance was established as a completely separate unit within the Royal Bank of Scotland to sell low-priced insurance over the telephone.

Even though this solution is quite efficient (and has been recognized as such for some time[15]), it is not problem-free. Once a separate unit has been set up, the challenge becomes how to manage the two so that they work together—for, rather than against, each other. Here again, what distinguishes successful innovators is not that they ask for integration. Rather, they create an organizational context (culture, structure, incentives, and people) that encourages and supports integration. (The same kind of organizational context discussed earlier, in Chapter 6, is used to achieve a desired behavior from employees.)

What kind of organizational context (or environment) promotes integration? At Leclerc, the strong family culture and the founder's motivating vision act as the glue that holds everything together; at Lan & Spar Bank, team-based incentives and rewards are regularly offered while information is allowed to flow quickly and uninterruptedly since no hierarchy exists; at Unilever, managers are often transferred across subsidiaries and national boundaries; at 3M cross-functional teams are regularly used, and information is shared at regular company conferences; at Bank One, "business integrators" travel from one branch to another, exchanging ideas and best practices. At Hewitt Associates, top management works continually at making sure that people *feel* and *see* the connections between the two businesses (consulting and administration) of the firm. The culture and the incentives of the organization prevent one group of employees from thinking they are better than or different from others.

In short, an organization can use an almost unlimited number of tactics and practices to achieve integration.[16] Usually, the problem is not lack of tactics or ideas—it is lack of will to put these tactics into practice.

Alternatively, when faced with a new strategic position, a firm may adopt it without intending its peaceful coexistence with the firm's current position. Recognizing the new position as the wave of the future, the company may choose to abandon the status quo in favor of it. The challenge here is how to manage the transition from the old to the new.

This transition challenge is far more demanding than the admittedly difficult integration challenge. As mentioned above, many companies fail when they attempt to respond to a technological innovation that seems to be taking over the market because they wait too long before responding. Yet another reason why they fail is that they manage the organizational transition from the "old" to the "new" ineffectively. This problem is illustrated in the following comment made by the CEO of a British bank. When confronted with the question of why his bank was not embracing the wave of direct banking that is sweeping the Western world, his frustrated reply was, "I see that direct banking is the future. But what do you want me to do—shut down 1,000 branches and fire 20,000 people overnight?"

His answer to this dilemma—not unlike that of most corporate executives—is to move from the old to the new *slowly*. Let the two systems coexist, but over time allocate more and more resources to the new so that it grows at the expense of the old. This approach minimizes the trauma of change, but it comes with issues of its own. The single biggest problem is that it allows the supporters of the status quo—or the managers whose interests lie with the status quo—to organize themselves and sabotage the transition. Only strong leadership from the top can surmount that possibility. Generating emotional commitment to the new strategic position, by convincing the organization of its need and importance, can also help the transition process.

The need to make a slow transition from one strategy to another implies that for a certain period of time, a firm has to live with two strategies playing out simultaneously. As already stated, managing parallel strategies is difficult. Lan & Spar tried it in 1990–93. While continuing to offer its traditional services (that is, normal products at normal prices) through the branch network, it also put into place a telephone banking offering. The two distribution methods were merged into the direct bank concept in 1993, but the firm still had to manage the transition between 1990 and 1993, when both the traditional and the new strategies were operational. According to CEO Peter Schou, this was an extremely demanding task. The difficulty lies in the necessity of maintaining one set of organizational structures, processes, and incentives in support of one strategy and another complete set of organizational structures and processes in support of the other. It is this need to be "ambidextrous" that is the real challenge. Companies that achieve ambidexterity can really claim to have achieved dynamic fit with their environment.

Summary

1. At any given time, numerous entrepreneurs are trying a variety of pursuits and are creating all kinds of niches on the periphery of any business. The problem is that while all this is happening, it is not clear which of these many niches will grow and emerge as a sizable strategic position.

2. Established companies should not allow this uncertainty to paralyze them, nor should they rush haphazardly into any new position. They should conduct a detailed cost/benefit analysis to determine whether to adopt a particular strategic position.

3. Because new positions are often in conflict with existing positions, the best way for an established competitor to adopt another position is by creating a separate organizational unit.

4. If a firm adopts a new strategic position with the idea of ultimately establishing it as its primary strategic position, the best course of action is to slowly phase out the older position.

10

Take a Dynamic View of Strategy

If you are going to cannibalize someone, you might as well cannibalize someone in the family.

—Craig Barrett, President of Intel

It is fair to say that despite the obvious importance of a superior strategy to the success of an organization and despite decades of academic research on the subject, there is surprisingly little agreement as to what strategy really is. Within business and academic circles alike, it would be quite miraculous to find two people who share the same definition of strategy. From notions of "strategy as positioning" to "strategy as visioning," several possible definitions are fighting for legitimacy. The lack of a generally accepted definition has led to an onslaught of "sexy" slogans and terms, all of which simply compound the confusion. No wonder a recent article in the *Economist* made the claim, "Nobody really knows what strategy is."[1]

Similar confusion and disagreements also surround the process for developing good strategies. The claim has been made that we are all experts after the fact in identifying companies with superior strategies, but we have little to say about how these superior strategies were created in the first place or how other companies could develop similarly innovative strategies.[2] For example, the debate that has been raging in the field for the past twenty years is whether a company can proactively choose its strategy through a process of rational thinking or whether it must allow its strategy to "emerge" through a process of experimentation.

To make matters worse, strategic thinking and advice have traditionally failed to take a dynamic view of strategy—that is, we have offered strategic advice and prescriptions without putting a firm in its historical context. Yet the right strategy for any firm must account for its unique evolution as well as the evolution of its industry. No single strategy can be the best one for every firm in every industry.

As a result of their being ahistorical, it is not unusual to hear academics and consultants offer the business community conflicting and even contradictory advice. Examples abound. Following the success of Thomas J. Peters and Robert H. Waterman's book *In Search of Excellence*, companies were advised to "stick to their knitting."[3] Yet, in a study of technological innovations, another consultant from the same firm as these two authors suggested that the last thing a company wants to do is stick to its knitting![4] In times of technological upheaval in your industry, sticking to your knitting is likely to land you in bankruptcy. Similarly, Harvard professor Ted Levitt argued in his influential article "Marketing Myopia" that companies should define their business broadly—not according to the product they are selling but according to the underlying functionality of their products.[5] Yet a second prominent academic, Hermann Simon, in *The Hidden Champions*, found that the German companies he had studied succeeded precisely because they were careful not to define their markets too broadly. Instead, they focused on narrow markets (which were defined according to the product they were selling) and then proceeded to dominate these markets worldwide.[6] Another example: A well-known marketing dictum says companies should listen to their customers; how many times have you heard, "The customer is always right"? Yet the authors of an award-winning article in the *Harvard Business Review* argued that companies that pay too much attention to their existing customers at times of technological change will fail.[7]

These examples show that no advice—however sound and practical—can apply to all firms, all the time. The actions a firm takes should grow out of its own particular circumstances, which are determined by its particular evolution. Strategic advice that fails to put the company in its historical context can be dangerous advice.

The Essence of Strategy

Strategy and the art and craft of creating it need not be so confusing. In this book, I have tried to push aside the rhetoric and jargon clouding the notion of strategy and get to the heart of the matter. In essence, crafting a strategy involves three steps (see Exhibit 10-1):

1. Generating as many ideas as possible about who to target, what to sell, and how to accomplish this.

2. Selecting from this set of ideas the ones the firm will pursue and discarding the ideas it will *not* pursue.

3. Implementing the selected idea(s) while remaining flexible to changes in the environment outside the firm.

Maximizing the Ideas Generated

It has often been said that pursuing a strategy involves making choices. A firm cannot make or do everything any more than it can target everyone—it simply doesn't have the resources. Of course, in order to make choices, the firm must have options from which to choose. And the more the better. The more creative a firm can be at the "idea-generation" stage of strategy making, the higher the probability that it will end up with a truly innovative strategy—one that breaks the rules of the game. Therefore, the first task in developing strategy must be to generate as many ideas as possible.

Throughout this book, and especially in Chapter 7, I have argued that numerous tactics can be employed to enhance creativity at this level. I have specifically proposed the following:

• Encourage everyone in the organization to question the firm's implicit assumptions and beliefs (that is, the firm's mental models) as to who your customers really are, what you are really offering those customers, and how you carry out these activities. Also encourage a deep questioning of the firm's accepted answer to "What business are we in?"

• To facilitate this questioning, create a positive crisis. If done correctly, this will galvanize the organization into active thinking. If done incorrectly, it will demoralize your staff and create confusion and disillusionment throughout the organization.

Exhibit 10-1 The Process of Crafting Breakthrough Strategy

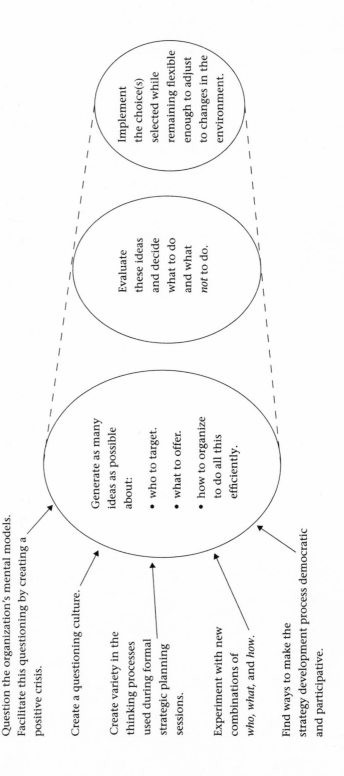

Question the organization's mental models. Facilitate this questioning by creating a positive crisis.

Create a questioning culture.

Create variety in the thinking processes used during formal strategic planning sessions.

Experiment with new combinations of *who, what,* and *how.*

Find ways to make the strategy development process democratic and participative.

Generate as many ideas as possible about:

- who to target.
- what to offer.
- how to organize to do all this efficiently.

Evaluate these ideas and decide what to do and what *not* to do.

Implement the choice(s) selected while remaining flexible enough to adjust to changes in the environment.

- Develop processes that encourage everyone involved with the organization—from employees to customers and distributors—to contribute strategic ideas and that ensure management will give these ideas a fair hearing. Recall the decatable approach at Lan & Spar Bank and the internal venturing unit at Schlumberger. Bank One has a specific center that customers are encouraged to call to express their complaints. My local supermarket has a customer suggestion box. Different organizations have come up with different approaches, but the idea is the same: Allow everybody to contribute ideas, and make it easy for them to communicate those ideas to the decision makers.

- Create variety in the thinking that takes place in formal planning. This can be achieved not only by putting together a diverse team but also by starting the process at different points. As described in Chapter 7, one way to do this is by taking your team through a number of exercises, all of which tackle the same issue from different angles.

- Institutionalize a culture of innovation. As discussed in Chapter 6, the company must create an organizational environment (as defined by its culture, structure, incentives, and people) that promotes and supports innovative behaviors.

Of course, when employing these techniques or others in the pursuit of an innovative strategy, the ultimate goal is to answer those three basic questions: who is the customer, what is the product or service, and how will the firm organize its operations so that it can reach its selected customers with its selected product or service.

Making Hard Choices

Having developed a long list of ideas about what it might want to do, the firm needs to decide what it actually will do. This means that every idea must be evaluated and choices made as to what and what not to pursue.

Making such choices is difficult. At the decision point, no one knows for sure whether a particular idea will work out or whether it is the best and most appropriate for the future of the firm. The uncertainty inherent in this stage can be reduced somewhat by establishing a rigorous evaluation process (using the evaluation criteria developed in Chapter 7) and/or by experimenting with the idea in a limited way to see how it works. However, it is crucial to understand that uncertainty cannot be eliminated altogether. No matter how much careful thought goes into evaluation or how much experimentation is carried out, the time will come when the firm must make a decision, one way or another. Lack of certainty is no excuse for indecision.

The firm must decide not only what it will do but also what it will *not* do. If management proclaims that the firm will pursue option A, then it shouldn't pursue option B in the name of keeping its options open. It has to be willing and able to close off some of the exits. To do otherwise is to shortchange not only both options but also the firm and its employees.

Implementing the Selected Strategy

Implementing a new strategy takes time. One reason is that any new strategy must be *sold* (not just communicated) to all the employees. Selling the new strategy to employees so as to win their emotional commitment is probably one of the most demanding and time-consuming tasks of leadership. I recommended an approach to this task in Chapter 5, but the point to keep in mind is that without the employees' emotional commitment to the new strategy, it is destined to fail.

In addition, the firm must develop the appropriate organizational environment to support the new strategy. As explained in Chapter 6, the organizational environment is composed of four elements: culture, structure, incentives, and people. Not only must each element support the selected strategy, but each element must also support and reinforce the others.

Finally, implementation can take time because experimentation may be necessary to determine if some of the decisions made actually work in the marketplace. From experimentation comes additional information that can help management decide whether its choices are working well or whether it needs to modify them. As described in Chapter 7, the evaluate/experiment/learn/modify stage can be time-consuming, but in may instances it is an absolute necessity if the firm is to avoid making costly mistakes.

In crafting and implementing a new strategy, the firm's goal should be to create a number of "fits." The four elements that make up the firm's organizational environment must fit with and reinforce one another while at the same time supporting and promoting the firm's chosen strategy. In addition, the choices the firm makes in determining its strategy (what customers to target, what products to sell, what activities to perform) must support and reinforce one another while at the same time allowing the firm to do exactly what is needed in its industry environment. The difficulty lies not so much in designing the individual pieces of this elaborate mosaic but in assembling them in a manner that will achieve and sustain these internal and external fits.

Simultaneous with creating the requisite fit with its current industry environment, the firm must build in enough flexibility to respond to changes in that environment. As explained in Chapter 4, the firm's agility in that regard generally hinges on three things: its ability to identify the changes early enough to do something about them, its cultural willingness to accept change, and its possession of the competencies necessary to compete in whatever environment emerges after the change.

A firm must institutionalize this kind of flexibility (in the manner described in Chapter 4) because the environment around it is continually changing, requiring continual responses and adjustments from the firm. Nowhere is this flexibility more needed than when the firm is confronted with a strategic innovation in its business—that is, the emergence of a new strategic position. A new strategic position is a new who/what/how combination that surfaces because of changing customer preferences, changing technologies, changing competitive moves, and so on. As explained in Chapters 8 and 9, new strategic positions constantly emerge on the periphery of industries. These entrants have the potential to grow and to erode the profitability of existing strategic positions. Thus, while vying with competitors in its current position, an established firm must also be on the lookout for new strategic positions it can and should colonize. Chapter 9 described how this can be achieved.

The Dynamism of Strategy

Having reviewed the essential components of strategy making, we can now construct a complete picture of a dynamic strategy (see Exhibit 10-2). In developing its strategy, a company must be prepared to go through the following cycle of thinking:

1. Begin by identifying and colonizing a *distinctive* strategic position in its industry.

2. Having carved out a unique position, play the game consummately well in that position so as to make it more attractive than all industry positions.

3. While fighting competitors in its current position, continually search for new strategic positions in its industry.

4. Having identified another viable strategic position, attempt to manage the "old" and the new positions simultaneously.

5. As the old position matures and declines over time, slowly make the transition to the new position and start the cycle all over again.

At any given time during this dynamic, the company can jump into a new technology or industry. This might happen early, while the company is still competing in its first strategic position, or later on, while the company is striving to balance the demands of two strategic positions, or at any time during the evolution of a firm's strategy. Making that leap triggers the cycle to begin again: Once more the firm must find itself a unique strategic position in the new industry, play the game exceedingly well in this position, search for and discover new strategic positions, and so on. Jumping into another business does not change the strategic tasks that a company must undertake. It just makes management a little more complicated by posing additional challenges, such as how to manage a diversified portfolio and how to exploit synergies among its businesses, or how to make a complete transition from one industry to another.

Thus, designing a successful strategy is a never-ending quest. Even the most successful companies must continually question the

Exhibit 10-2 Strategy as a Dynamic, Lifelong Process

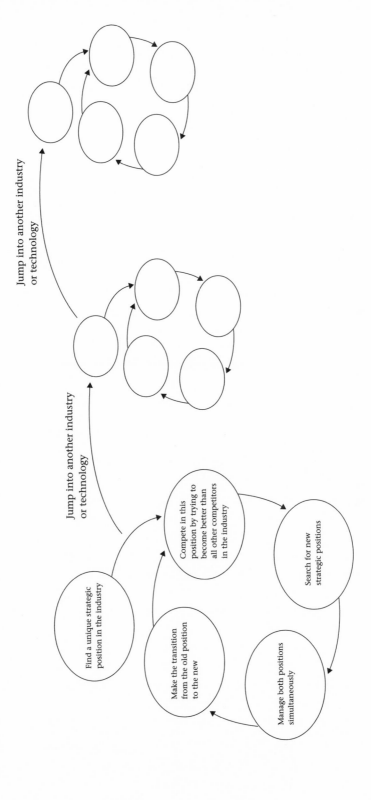

basis of their business and the assumptions underlying their "formula for success." (In fact, in one way or another, this is what most successful companies have done to get where they are.) New who/what/how positions are constantly popping up around the mass market, and established companies must be on the lookout for them. Like a modern-day Christopher Columbus, each company must set out to explore its industry's evolving terrain, searching for new and unexploited strategic positions. I hope that this book will provide you with a roadmap for this journey of discovery. Bon voyage!

Notes

Chapter 1 Put Innovation Back into Strategy

1. The who/what/how framework I'm proposing here was originally developed by Derek F. Abell in *Defining the Business: The Starting Point of Strategic Planning* (Englewood Cliffs, N.J.: Prentice-Hall, 1980).

2. Richard Teitelbaum, "Edward Jones: The Wal-Mart of Wall Street," *Fortune*, October 13, 1997, 70–72.

3. P. Weever, "Growing Call of Telephone Banks," *Sunday Telegraph* (London), 22 December 1996, 2, and A. Bailey, "Telephone Banking—It's for Your: The Service Has Scope for Great Popularity," *Financial Times*, 3 April 1996, 18.

4. John Seely Brown, "Research that Reinvents the Corporation," Harvard Business Review, January–February 1991, 102–111.

5. Edward W. Desmond: "Can Canon Keep Clicking?" *Fortune*, 2 February 1998, 58–64.

6. "K mart Has to Open Some New Doors on the Future," *Fortune*, July 1977, 144.

7. Erick Schonfeld, "Schwab Puts It All Online," *Fortune*, 7 December 1998, 64–68.

8. Robert A. Burgelman and Andrew S. Grove, "Strategic Dissonance," *California Management Review* 38, no. 2 (Winter 1996): 15.

9. Nancy O. Perry, "Snapshot: Gary DiCamillo, Polaroid's CEO," *Harvard Business School Bulletin*, April 1998, 19.

10. If this happens, value will migrate from one strategic position to another; see the excellent study by Adrian J. Slywotzky, *Value Migration: How to Think Several Moves Ahead of the Competition* (Boston: Harvard Business School Press, 1996).

Chapter 2 Decide What Your Business Is

1. I have replicated this "experiment" with exactly the same results with a variety of audiences, ranging from high school students to senior managers.

2. See James Walsh, "Managerial and Organizational Cognition: Notes from a Trip Down Memory Lane," *Organizational Science* 6, no. 3 (May–June 1995): 280–321.

3. Good discussions of mental models and ways to escape them can be found in J. C. Spender, *Industry Recipes: An Enquiry into the Nature and Sources of Managerial Judgement* (Oxford: Basil Blackwell, 1990), and in Peter Grinyer and

Peter McKiernan, "Triggering Major and Sustained Changes in Stagnating Companies," in *Strategic Groups, Strategic Moves and Performance*, 173–195, ed. Herman Daems and Howard Thomas (New York: Pergamon, 1994). A very practical discussion of these issues is found in Joel Arthur Barker, *Paradigms: The Business of Discovering the Future* (New York: HarperBusiness, 1993).

4. Quoted from the 1997 Stockton Lecture delivered at London Business School by Andrew Grove. The full text of the speech is published as "Navigating Strategic Inflection Points," *Business Strategy Review* 8, no. 3 (Autumn 1997): 11–18.

5. See my book *Diversification, Refocusing, and Economic Performance* (Cambridge, Mass.: MIT Press, 1995). See also my article "To Diversify or Not to Diversify," *Harvard Business Review*, November–December 1997, 93–99.

6. The importance of starting the development of any new strategy by defining the business is demonstrated in Gary L. Frazier and Roy D. Howell, "Business Definition and Performance," *Journal of Marketing* 47 (Spring 1983): 59–67; Geoffrey R. Brooks, "Defining Market Boundaries," *Strategic Management Journal* 16 (1995): 535–549; and John Nightingale, "On the Definition of "Industry" and "Market," *Journal of Industrial Economics* 27 (September 1978): 31–40.

7. Hal Rosenbluth, "Tales from a Nonconformist Company," *Harvard Business Review*, July–August 1991, 26–36.

8. Ibid.

9. Ibid.

10. Charles McCoy, "Entrepreneur Smells Aroma of Success in Coffee Bars," *Wall Street Journal*, 8 January 1993.

11. See in particular Gary Hamel and C. K. Prahalad, *Competing for the Future* (Boston: Harvard Business School Press, 1994), 83.

12. Hermann Simon, *Hidden Champions: Lessons from 500 of the World's Best Unknown Companies* (Boston: Harvard Business School Press, 1996).

13. A long list of the criteria that can be used to evaluate alternative business definitions can be found in Abell, *Defining the Business*, 179–184. Another look at the same issue from a different angle is provided by George Day, "Assessing Competitive Arenas: Who Are Your Competitors?" in *Wharton on Dynamic Competitive Strategy*, 26–33, ed. George Day and David Reibstein (New York: John Wiley and Sons, 1997). The approach adopted in that essay, which is the approach recommended in the marketing literature in general, is to view as competitors those companies which produce products that are close substitutes for your products. Because there are many ways to measure degree of substitutability (for instance, substitutes in kind, substitutes in use, substitutes in production), there may be many ways to define your business. My argument here is that degree of substitutability is only *one* of the criteria a company must consider in the process of defining its business.

14. "Texas Instruments Shows U.S. Business How to Survive in the 1980s," *Business Week*, 18 September 1978, 66–72.

Chapter 3   Decide Who Your Customers Are and What to Offer Them

1. Interview with Michael Porter in the video *Michael Porter on Competitive Strategy* (Boston: Harvard Business School Publishing Corporation, 1988).

2. Skil was eventually acquired by the German firm Bosch.

3. The issue of segmentation is covered thoroughly in most marketing texts. See, for example, George Day, *Market-Driven Strategy: Processes for Creating Value* (New York: Free Press, 1990). I will not cover this issue at any length.

4. "America's Car-Rental Business: Driven into the Ground," *The Economist*, 20 January 1996, 76–79.

5. According to Gary Hamel, separating form from function (that is, looking at the underlying functionality of the product) is one way for companies to achieve industry revolution. See Gary Hamel, "Strategy as Revolution," *Harvard Business Review*, July–August 1996, 69–82.

6. Grove, Stockton Lecture.

7. Gary Hamel, "Killer Strategies That Make Shareholders Happy," *Fortune*, 23 June 1997, 32.

8. Henry Mintzberg, "Crafting Strategy," *Harvard Business Review*, July–August 1987, 68.

9. Burgelman and Grove, "Strategic Dissonance."

10. The importance of monitoring not only changing customer needs but also shifting customer priorities is discussed in more detail by Hiroyuki Itami in *Mobilizing Invisible Assets* (Cambridge, Mass.: Harvard University Press, 1987). See Chapter 3 and especially pp. 40–49.

11. Charles A. Jaffe, "Moving Fast by Standing Still," *Nation's Business*, October 1991, 58.

12. The need to pick the "right" niche is also raised by Gerard Tellis and Peter Golder, "First to Market, First to Fail? Real Causes of Enduring Market Leadership," *Sloan Management Review* 37, no. 2 (Winter 1996): 65–75. Their argument is that "strategic innovators" have a vision of the mass market and that they actively try to produce quality products at low prices to appeal to that mass market. Thus, the secret of their success is the fact that they target the mass market and succeed in serving it. Although I agree with the point, my research suggests that luck, good timing, and external events should not be underestimated as important ingredients in the success of strategic innovators to "pick" the right niche at the right time.

13. William Taylor, "The Business of Innovation: An Interview with Paul Cook," *Harvard Business Review*, March–April 1990, 97–106.

14. There is a vast literature on the usefulness, as well as the limits, of "getting close to the customer." See, in particular, Stuart Macdonald, "Too Close for Comfort? The Strategic Implications of Getting Close to the Customer," *California Management Review* 37, no. 4 (Summer 1995): 8–27, and Itamar Simonson, "Get Closer to Your Customers by Understanding How They Make Choices," *California Management Review* 35, no. 4 (Summer 1993): 68–84.

15. Kenichi Ohmae, "Getting Back to Strategy," *Harvard Business Review*, November–December 1988, 149–156.

16. "What Makes Yoshio Invent," *The Economist*, 12 January 1991, 61.

17. Gary Hamel and C. K. Prahalad, "Corporate Imagination and Expeditionary Marketing," *Harvard Business Review*, July–August 1991, 81–92.

18. William Davidson, "You Can Have It All," *Fortune*, 4 March 1996, 93.

19. An excellent discussion on how to leverage core competencies into new products or new ways of competing is found in C. K. Prahalad and Gary

Hamel, "The Core Competence of the Corporation," *Harvard Business Review*, May–June 1990, 79–91.

20. Thomas Steward, "3M Fights Back," *Fortune*, 5 February 1996, 44.

21. Hamel and Prahalad, "Corporate Imagination and Expeditionary Marketing," 81–92.

22. A good discussion of how to improve corporate creativity is found on pp. 83–86 of Hamel and Prahalad, "Corporate Imagination and Expeditionary Marketing." The authors argue that "four elements combine to quicken a company's corporate imagination: escaping the tyranny of served markets; searching for innovative product concepts; overturning traditional assumptions about price/performance relationships; and leading customers rather than simply following them."

Chapter 4   Decide How You Will Play the Game

1. The idea that the firm is a complex system of interrelationships that should be viewed and managed as such is one of the founding principles of "system dynamics" as developed by MIT's Jay W. Forrester. A powerful and managerial exposition of system dynamics and systems-thinking principles can be found in Peter M. Senge, *The Fifth Discipline: The Art and Practice of the Learning Organization* (New York: Doubleday/Currency, 1990). See also David E. Meen and Mark Keough, "Creating the Learning Organization: An Interview with Peter Senge," in *The McKinsey Quarterly Anthologies: Business Dynamics*, 79–93 (New York: McKinsey and Co., 1997), and "The CEO as Organization Designer: An Interview with Professor Jay W. Forrester," *McKinsey Quarterly*, no. 2 (1992): 3–30.

2. The idea that companies need to organize so as to manage incremental and revolutionary change simultaneously is discussed at length in Michael Tushman and Charles O'Reilly III, "The Ambidextrous Organization: Managing Evolutionary and Revolutionary Change," *California Management Review* 38, no. 4 (Summer 1996): 1–23.

3. The original experiment was conducted by Professors David Aaker and Kevin Lane Keller, who present their results in the article "Consumer Evaluations of Brand Extensions," *Journal of Marketing* 54 (January 1990): 27–41. The results presented here are based on a series of experiments I carried out with 120 executives attending the Accelerated Development Program at London Business School in the period 1993–96.

4. This point is also made by Michael Porter in his article "What Is Strategy?" *Harvard Business Review*, November–December 1996, 61–78.

5. This is especially the case if we are under time pressure: people under pressure forget that they are part of a larger whole. Under pressure we focus on managing our own piece of the system. As I will argue later, this does not work because of interrelationships in the system.

6. Additional insights on how systems thinking can be used in companies can be found in John Morecroft, "The Feedback View of Business Policy and Strategy," *System Dynamics Review* 36, no. 1 (Summer 1985): 4–19; John Morecroft and John Sterman, eds., *Modeling for Learning Organizations* (Portland, Ore.: Productivity Press, 1994); and Senge, *The Fifth Discipline*.

7. See Meen and Keough, "An Interview with Peter Senge."

8. As indicated, the literature on this topic is extensive. As a start, readers are referred to Robert A. Burgelman and Leonard R. Sayles, *Inside Corporate Innovation: Strategy, Structure, and Managerial Skills* (New York: Free Press, 1986); Rosabeth Moss Kanter, *The Change Masters: Innovation and Entrepreneurship in the American Corporation* (New York: Simon & Schuster, 1984); Michael Tushman and William Moore, eds., *Readings in the Management of Innovation*, 2d ed. (New York: HarperBusiness, 1988); Danny Miller, "The Icarus Paradox: How Exceptional Companies Bring About Their Own Downfall," *Business Horizons* 35, no. 1 (1992): 24–35; and Sumantra Ghoshal and Christopher Bartlett, "Changing the Role of Top Management: Beyond Structure to Processes," *Harvard Business Review*, January–February 1995, 86–96.

9. Similar concepts can be found in Charles Handy, *The Empty Raincoat* (London: Basic Books, 1994); C. Markides: "Business Is Good? Time for Change!" (London Business School) *Alumni News*, Spring 1994, 15; and Burgelman and Grove, "Strategic Dissonance."

10. Tim Smart, "Jack Welch's Encore," *Business Week*, 28 October 1996, 154–160.

11. Linda Grant, "Outmarketing P&G," *Fortune*, 12 January 1988, 68–70.

12. The importance of monitoring the organization's strategic health so as to anticipate (rather than react to) change is also emphasized in Charles Baden-Fuller and John M. Stopford, *Rejuvenating the Mature Business: The Competitive Challenge* (Boston: Harvard Business School Press, 1994); M. Tushman, W. Newman, and E. Romanelli, "Convergence and Upheaval: Managing the Unsteady Pace of Organizational Evolution," *California Management Review* 26, no. 1 (Fall 1986): 29–44; and C. Markides, "Strategic Management: An Overview," in the *"Financial Times" Handbook of Management*, 126–135, ed. Stuart Crainer (London: Financial Times Pitman Publishing, 1995).

13. A fuller discussion of these issues can be found in Robert S. Kaplan and David P. Norton, *The Balanced Scorecard: Translating Strategy into Action* (Boston: Harvard Business School Press, 1996).

14. See, for example, Gary Hamel and C. K. Prahalad, "Strategic Intent," *Harvard Business Review*, May–June 1989, 63–76, and James C. Collins and Jerry I. Porras, *Built to Last: Successful Habits of Visionary Companies* (New York: HarperBusiness, 1994).

15. Richard Nelson, "Capitalism as an Engine of Progress," *Research Policy* 19 (1990): 193–214.

16. Eric D. Beinhocker, "Strategy at the Edge of Chaos," *McKinsey Quarterly*, no. 1 (1997): 34.

17. For a supporting discussion, see Tushman and O'Reilly III, "The Ambidextrous Organization"; Burgelman and Grove, "Strategic Dissonance," *California Management Review* 38, no. 2 (Winter 1996): 8–28; and Bartlett and Ghoshal, "Changing the Role of Top Management."

Chapter 5   Identify and Secure Strategic Assets and Capabilities

1. This point is discussed in detail in Paul Verdin and Peter Williamson, "Successful Strategy: Stargazing or Self-Examination?" *European Management Journal* 12, no. 1 (March 1994): 10–19.

2. See, for example, Jay B. Barney, "Looking Inside for Competitive Advantage," *Academy of Management Executive* 9, no. 4 (1995): 49–61.

3. Ibid., 53.

4. Ibid., 56.

5. For a detailed discussion on how to create a learning organization, see Ikujiro Nonaka and Hirotaka Takeuchi, *The Knowledge-Creating Company: How Japanese Companies Create the Dynamics of Innovation* (New York: Oxford University Press, 1995). See also Ikujiro Nonaka, "The Knowledge-Creating Company," *Harvard Business Review*, November–December 1991, 96–104, and David A. Garvin, "Building a Learning Organization," *Harvard Business Review*, July–August 1993, 78–91.

6. Christopher A. Bartlett, "McKinsey & Company: Managing Knowledge and Learning," Case 396-397 (Boston: Harvard Business School, 1996).

7. The concept of the strategic staircase can be credited to Michael Hay and Peter Williamson, "Strategic Staircases: Planning the Capabilities Required for Success," *Long Range Planning* 24, no. 4 (August 1991): 36–43.

8. George Gendron, "The Art of Loving," *Inc.*, May 1989.

9. Hay and Williamson, "Strategic Staircase."

Chapter 6 Create the Right Organizational Environment

1. The notion that the underlying "structure" of a system creates the behavior in that system has been the subject of much literature in the systems dynamics field. See, for example, J. Forrester, *Principles of Systems*, 2d ed. (Portland, Ore.: Productivity Press, 1968), and A. Van Ackere, E. Larsen, and J. Morecroft, "Systems Thinking and Business Process Redesign," *European Management Journal* 11, no. 4 (1993): 412–423. For a more managerial angle, see C. Bartlett and S. Ghoshal, "Rebuilding Behavioral Context: Turn Process Reengineering into People Reengineering," *Sloan Management Review* 37, no. 1 (Fall 1995): 11–23.

2. A detailed discussion of how the underlying environment conditions behavior and how to design an environment for strategic renewal can be found in Robert Simons, *Levers of Control: How Managers Use Innovative Control Systems to Drive Strategic Renewal* (Boston: Harvard Business School Press, 1995).

3. The beer game is described in more detail in Chapter 3 of Peter Senge's *The Fifth Discipline*.

4. Senge, *The Fifth Discipline*, 42.

5. See, for example, Ann van Ackere, Erik Reimer Larsen, and John Morecroft, "Systems Thinking and Business Process Redesign: An Application to the Beer Game," *European Management Journal* 11, no. 4 (1993): 412–423.

6. An excellent account of how to create an underlying environment that promotes desired behaviors on the part of employees can be found in Sumantra Ghoshal and Christopher A. Bartlett, *The Individualized Corporation: A Fundamentally New Approach to Management* (New York: HarperBusiness, 1997).

7. What I am calling *organizational environment* is what is widely known as the 7S framework developed by McKinsey & Company. The seven Ss are style, strategy, structure, systems, skills, staff, and superordinate goals.

8. The quotes come from Taylor, "Interview with Paul Cook."

9. The importance of putting properly selected individual parts together to form a strong and reinforcing system is made forcefully and in much more detail in David A. Nadler and Michael L. Tushman, *Competing by Design: The Power of Organizational Architecture* (New York: Oxford University Press, 1997).

10. A change in the external environment (either continuous or discontinuous) is only one reason why a nice fit may suddenly become a misfit. Another common reason is the evolution of a company from one stage of its development to another (e.g., from entrepreneurial to mature and professional or from domestic to multinational).

11. William M. Carley, "Bumpy Flights—Many Travelers Gripe about People Express Citing Overbooking," *Wall Street Journal*, 19 May 1986, 1.

12. For a practical discussion on how to change an organization's underlying environment, see Chapter 10 of Nadler and Tushman, *Competing by Design*.

Chapter 7   Develop a Superior Strategic Position

1. See, for example, Gary Hamel, "Strategy Innovation and the Quest for Value," *Sloan Management Review* 39, no. 2 (Winter 1998): 7–14.

2. Ian C. MacMillan and Rita Gunther McGrath, letter published in *Harvard Business Review*, January–February 1997, 154–156, in response to Michael Porter's article "What Is Strategy?"

3. Gary S. Lynn, Joseph G. Morone, and Albert S. Paulson, "Marketing and Discontinuous Innovation: The Probe and Learn Process," *California Management Review* 38, no. 3 (Spring 1996): 8–37.

4. Variants of this approach are described in Rita Gunther McGrath and Ian C. MacMillan, "Discovery-Driven Planning," *Harvard Business Review*, July–August 1995, 44–54; Lynn, Morone, and Paulson, "Marketing and Discontinuous Innovation"; Hamel and Prahalad, "Corporate Imagination and Expeditionary Marketing"; and Clayton Christensen, "Discovering New and Emerging Markets," in Chapter 7 of *The Innovator's Dilemma: When New Technologies Cause Great Firms to Fail* (Boston: Harvard Business School Press, 1997).

5. Morone and Paulson, "Marketing and Discontinuous Innovation."

6. Ibid.

7. Christensen, "Discovering New and Emerging Markets."

8. "How Can Big Companies Keep the Entrepreneurial Spirit Alive?" *Harvard Business Review*, November–December 1995, 183–192.

Chapter 8   Understand How New Strategic Positions Develop

1. There is only one major exception to this generalization: in cases when the attacker utilizes a dramatic technological innovation to attack the leader, seven of ten market leaders lose out. See the fascinating study by James M. Utterback, *Mastering the Dynamics of Innovation* (Boston: Harvard Business School Press, 1994).

2. S. Davies, P. Geroski, M. Lund, and A. Vlassopoulos, "The Dynamics of Market Leadership in the U.K. Manufacturing Industry, 1979–1986," working

paper 93, Centre for Business Strategy, London Business School, 1991, and P. Geroski and S. Toker, "The Turnover of Market Leaders in U.K. Manufacturing: 1979–1986" (London Business School, 1993, mimeographed).

Chapter 9   Evaluate and Respond to Strategic Innovation

1. In 1997 alone, *Harvard Business Review* published two articles on this topic, as did the *Sloan Management Review*. The cover story in the 23 June 1997 issue of *Fortune* magazine was about strategic innovation. In it, the strategies of companies that have succeeded by breaking the rules (Southwest Airlines, CNN, Wal-Mart, Body Shop, Dell, Nucor, Starbucks, IKEA, Home Depot, and the like) were cited as examples for corporate America to emulate.

2. Ronald B. Lieber, ""Who Are the Real Wealth Creators?" *Fortune*, 9 December 1996, 61–66, and Melanie Warner, "Size Matters," *Fortune*, 28 April 1997, 116–117.

3. See my article "Strategic Innovation," *Sloan Management Review* 38, no. 3 (Spring 1997): 9–23.

4. The answer, according to Michael Porter, is no. In his article "What Is Strategy?" Porter describes how Continental Airlines tried to play both games by maintaining its position as a full-service airline while creating a new service dubbed Continental Lite to imitate the strategy of Southwest. This venture failed, suggesting that "[positioning trade-offs] deter straddling or repositioning, because competitors that engage in those approaches undermine their strategies and degrade the value of their existing activities" (p. 69).

5. For a fascinating discussion on how IBM, Compaq, and HP are trying to imitate Dell's position (without abandoning their own), see David Kirkpatrick, "Now Everyone in PCs Wants to Be Like Mike," *Fortune*, 8 September 1997, 47–48. Earlier attempts by IBM to play both games simultaneously (through a direct-sales operation called Ambra) failed.

6. In fact, British Airways announced in November 1997 that it had decided to do exactly this! A separate subsidiary called Go has been set up and is now competing directly with easyJet in the low-cost segment of the market.

7. See Porter, "What Is Strategy?"

8. Seely Brown, "Research That Reinvents the Corporation."

9. A. Cooper and C. Smith, "How Established Firms Respond to Threatening Technologies," *Academy of Management Executive* 6, no. 2 (1992): 55–70; Richard N. Foster, *Innovation: The Attacker's Advantage* (New York: Summit Books, 1986); A. Cooper and D. Schendel, "Strategic Responses to Technological Threats," *Business Horizons*, February 1976, 61–69; and Utterback, *Mastering the Dynamics of Innovation*.

10. Beinhocker, "Strategy at the Edge of Chaos."

11. Ronald Henkoff, "Growing Your Company: Five Ways to Do It Right!" *Fortune*, 25 November 1996, 38.

12. The need to balance the old with the new is also discussed by Tushman and O'Reilly in "The Ambidextrous Organization" and by Burgelman and Grove in "Strategic Dissonance."

13. Tushman and O'Reilly, "The Ambidextrous Organization," 11.

14. Utterback, *Mastering the Dynamics of Innovation*, 216.

15. See, for example, Burgelman and Sayles, *Inside Corporate Innovation*.

16. See, for example, S. Ghoshal and C. Bartlett, "Rebuilding Behavioral Context: A Blueprint for Corporate Renewal," *Sloan Management Review* 37, no. 2 (Winter 1996): 23–36.

Chapter 10   Take a Dynamic View of Strategy

1. "Business Strategy: Eenie, Meenie, Minie, Mo . . ." *The Economist*, 20 March 1993, 106.

2. See, for example, Gary Hamel, "The Search for Strategy," working paper, London Business School, 1996.

3. Thomas J. Peters and Robert H. Waterman, *In Search of Excellence* (New York: Harper & Row, 1982).

4. Richard J. Foster, *Innovation: The Attacker's Advantage* (New York: Summit Books, 1986).

5. Theodore Levitt, "Marketing Myopia," *Harvard Business Review*, July–August 1960, 45–56.

6. Simon, *Hidden Champions*.

7. Joseph L. Bower and Clayton M. Christensen, "Disruptive Technologies: Catching the Wave," *Harvard Business Review*, January–February 1995, 43–53.

Index

About the Author

Constantinos C. Markides is Professor of Strategic and International Management and Chairman of the Strategy Department at the London Business School. Previously, he was an Associate with the Cyprus Development Bank and a Research Associate at the Harvard Business School.

He has taught in many in-company programs (for firms including Unilever, British Aerospace, Pirelli, Avon, Honeywell, Wellcome, Polygram, James Capel, Mercury Asset Management, and Warner Lambert) and is on the Academic Advisory Board of the Cyprus International Institute of Management. He is also a nonexecutive Director of Amathus (U.K.) Ltd., a tour operating company.

Dr. Markides has done research and published on the topics of strategic innovation, corporate restructuring, refocusing, and international acquisitions. His current research interests include the management of diversified firms and the use of innovation and creativity to achieve strategic breakthroughs.

He is the author of *Diversification, Refocusing and Economic Performance* and many articles published in journals such as the *Harvard Business Review, Sloan Management Review, Directors*

& *Boards*, *Long Range Planning*, *British Journal of Management*, *Journal of International Business Studies*, *Strategic Management Journal*, and the *Academy of Management Journal*. He is the Associate Editor of the *European Management Journal* and a member of the editorial boards of the *Strategic Management Journal* and the *Academy of Management Journal*. He is also a Fellow of the World Economic Forum in Davos, Switzerland.